THE BLACK HAT CHEF COOKBOOK

THE BLACK HAT CHEF COOKBOOK

by Chef René

A Lou Reda Book

RICHARDSON & STEIRMAN, INC.
NEW YORK

Library of Congress Catalog Number: 87-062152

ISBN: 0-931933-53-6

FIRST EDITION

10 9 8 7 6 5 4 3 2 1

To my beloved wife, Ann, who (honestly) made me do this, and to my loving grandmother, who at age ninety-seven was still teaching me cooking tricks. She started my love for cooking when I was but six years old, and her Mohawk Indian teachings gave me the lust for life that I enjoy to this day.

ACKNOWLEDGMENTS

*H*undreds of people helped me get to where I am today. I want to thank so many, yet I get the feeling that I will miss some, so to them my sincere apologies.

First, I wish to honor the memory of my mentors from Les Chefs Internationale, The Black Hat Society: Joe Donon, Al Stockli, Patsy Mazzucelli, Papa Gino Leone, and Ted Baun.

Second, the old guard from the R.I. Professional Chefs Association: Gino Corelli, John Coressimo, Adolph Schrott, Charlie Arakalian, Bob Holland, Dick Roy, A. J. Morrone, and Dick Rampino.

To the new guard from the American Culinary Federation: Jeff Brooks, Michel Marcais, Paul Prudhomme, Emeril LaGasse, Mike Minor, Clarke Bernier, Robin Nixon, Mark Fitch, Joe Strangis, Stafford DeCambra, William Trask, Conrad Nonaka, Richard Reynolds, Wendell Rodrigues, Sam Choy, Maurice Fitzgerald, Carol Ann Reed, Debbie Kennedy, Susan Spicer, Leon Oppenheimer, Helmut Hamann, Al Constantine, Tom Bloodworth, Jason Kleinpeter, Jeff Smith, Phil Learned, Michel LeBorgne, George Karousos, Ted Butzbach, Bob Cribari, Johnny Rivers, Ruben Foster, Steve Pagano, Bert Cutino, Jack Braun, Fred Faria, John Bowen; the man who acts as our rep so well, Ed Brown; and, last but never least, for my respect for him is so great, chef Franz Lemoine. To these and to so many other members of this fantastic organization, for their continued contributions to the culinary field and for what they have come to mean to me, my most profound and humble thanks.

To those, also, from my new field, TV, who have also helped me: that fabulous Chinese chef-instructor, Martin Yan; the great Julia Child (and, no, it's not true, she never did drop a chicken on one of her shows); Roland, from Christian's in New Orleans, on the *Taste of New Orleans* shows; Jeff Smith, the Frugal Gourmet; and the one I have looked up to and whom I consider the best and a real friend, the former Galloping Gourmet, Graham Kerr—my sincerest thanks for all that you have taught me, given me, and done for me.

I want to give especial thanks to Sandy Richardson, my publisher, and Gilda Abramowitz, the editor of this book, for doing such a fantastic job, taking my jumbled array of mixed-up recipes and putting it together so beautifully.

Contents

Foreword

Without question, it was better to have met over a flat tire than a fallen soufflé.

I met Chef René (with black hat in place) over one such deflating experience (the tire, that is!). Our meeting was brief, but Richard is a colorful man, not easily forgotten. He is immediately personable.

His mark of friendship is his willingness to help. Richard is a natural born teacher. By carefully reading this book, you will learn the fine art of cooking from one of the most gifted and respected chefs.

Richard lives, cooks, and writes with intensity. His passion is absolute, his enthusiasm contagious. He really does want to be helpful. He has given his life in service, cooking for people who want good food. His techniques are professional and he communicates well.

Today, major changes are occurring in the style and manner of eating. Chef René gives you classic methods that stress essential flavor, and a presentation that lends itself equally to traditional dishes and the newer, lighter foods.

I'm truly honored to be his friend.

—Graham Kerr,
the former Galloping Gourmet

Introduction

A cookbook is nothing more than a guide to good eating—no more, no less. When it comes to cooking, the heart of the matter is not so much learning how to make certain dishes as how not to overseason, overcook, or overeat.

In using any cookbook, all you need to do is learn the ingredients, then approach the entire thing with a feeling of having made up the recipe yourself. Gain as much confidence as you possibly can, and remember, from the first, that you are the chef and the dish is to please you, not your guest or guests. After all, most of the time you are cooking to feed yourself and your family. Your taste is what really counts, so feel free to adjust the types and amounts of ingredients called for in a recipe. Make it yours.

Follow your instincts, make it taste the way you like, serve only the amount you feel is right, and you will seldom make mistakes.

From the Chef's Notebook

To core an apple that will be cooked whole, use a tool made just for that purpose—but if the apple is to be cut up, quarter it, then slice out the core with a paring knife.

If a stubborn jar top refuses to yield, turn the jar upside down, tap the cover around its edges, then just twist and off it comes.

Never use a damp towel or potholder to take a hot pot off the heat or out of the oven. Heat turns the moisture to scalding steam.

To get the maximum volume from eggs for soufflés or omelettes, separate them when they are cold and let them come to room temperature before whipping them up.

Lemons have innumerable uses. They are the finest of tenderizers for meats (papaya juice works well, too), and fish should never be served without them.

Got the smell of garlic or onions on your hands? Rub a cut lemon on them.

Want cut-up fresh fruit to keep its color? Soak it in water with some lemon juice in it. Add a dash of lemon juice (or vinegar) to the water when cooking beets or red cabbage; this helps keep it red.

If long-refrigerated lemons have dried out, simmer them in boiling water for a few minutes, then pierce one end and squeeze. You will be surprised at how much juice comes out.

The greatest marinade for meat is 1/4 cup lemon juice, 1/2 cup olive oil, 2 crushed garlic cloves, 1 finely chopped small onion, oregano, salt, and crushed pepper. To tenderize a cheap cut of meat, marinate it in papaya juice.

If you need softened butter, but forgot to take it out of the refrigerator or freezer, simply grate it. To serve butter decoratively for a special guest, whip it with a little cream and squeeze it out of a pastry tube with a star tip.

If cheese seems always to stick to the grater, rub oil on the grater first.

If you are planning to serve a soufflé but will be pressed for time, prepare it up to the point of adding the egg whites. At serving time, beat the egg whites, fold them in, and bake.

If you have trouble with soggy pie crusts, brush them with egg white and dust with flour. If it's only the bottom that gives you trouble, just dust it with flour and sugar.

If your soup is too salty, a peeled and quartered raw potato will absorb much of the excess.

There are many ways to rescue a curdled hollandaise. Take the pan off the heat and whisk in hot water, a spoonful at a time, until it regains its smoothness. Or take it off the heat, throw in a small handful of chipped ice, and whisk vigorously until smooth. Or take it off the heat and whisk in chilled cream. If none of these works, put it in a blender and homogenize it. This works every time.

If you are going to broil a great deal of food at once, put a few slices of dry bread under the rack. They will absorb most of the fat drippings and prevent smoking and possibly a fire.

To freshen the flavor of frozen vegetables, add a pinch of sugar to the cooking water.

If a sauce is somewhat lumpy or not as smooth as you would like, just strain it. If you want to thicken it, purée the solids and whisk in.

Most sauces should never be cooked above a simmer, especially butter sauces (which often are made with delicate egg yolks, too).

To make a gravy or sauce to accompany a pan-fried dish, pour a little champagne or club soda into the pan and scrape up the browned particles stuck to the bottom.

Do you often cook wild game? Use vinegar in the marinade or even just to wash off the game. It reduces the wild taste.

If your rice comes out sticky, try browning it first in oil or butter. This gives it a nutty flavor, too. To reheat rice, put it in a sieve over a pan of simmering water, cover it, and steam it for about 5 minutes.

Raisins and other fruit tend to sink to the bottom of cake batters. To prevent this, flour them before adding them to the batter.

Have trouble applying frosting to a cake? Dust the cake with a bit of flour or cornstarch first. If cake icings always seem to become grainy, add a pinch of salt. To keep icing moist, add a bit of baking powder to the confectioner's sugar.

A bouquet garni consists of herbs (1 marjoram sprig, 2 parsley sprigs, 2 thyme sprigs, 1 small bay leaf) wrapped in a piece of cheesecloth; it is dropped into the pot, then removed and thrown away when the cooking is done. Instead of cheesecloth, you can put the herbs in an aluminum tea ball—cheap and reusable.

Chocolate can be tricky to work with. The next time you have to melt some, grease the pan first. The chocolate will pour out more easily and less of it will stick to the pan.

For an easy dessert, dip the ends of strawberries, grapes, or other fruit in melted chocolate, chill on a rack in the refrigerator, and serve with cheeses and/or champagne or wine.

If you are like me, you always have trouble with the membrane of an orange—you know, the white part that sticks to the part you want to eat. To get around that, soak the orange in hot water for about 5 minutes, then peel it. Refrigerate it to the desired serving temperature.

Uh-oh—you whipped heavy cream too much and it turned to butter. To rescue it, add a bit of milk and beat it in very carefully. It will turn back into whipped cream.

Speaking of whipping, you can whisk for a long time without getting tired if you alter your grip. Use a thick-handled whisk; instead of grasping it from above, hold it against your palm, between the thumb and forefinger, with the thumb standing up and the forefinger bent down. Use the other three fingers to snap the whisk handle repeatedly against your palm.

Sometimes you reach for an ingredient only to find that you are out of it. These substitutes can be used without altering the flavor of the dish: To replace 1 cup buttermilk, add 1 tablespoon vinegar or lemon juice to 1 cup milk and let stand for 5 minutes. Instead of sour cream, add a bit of vinegar or lemon juice to sweet cream and let stand for an hour (or use plain yogurt). For corn syrup, substitute sugar plus more of the liquid called for in the recipe. You can use undiluted evaporated milk instead of light cream. To replace 1 tablespoon baking powder, use 1 teaspoon baking soda plus 2 teaspoons cream of tartar. To replace 1 tablespoon flour for thickening, use 1/2 tablespoon cornstarch or 2 teaspoons quick-cooking tapioca.

Do not salt vegetables too soon before serving or they will lose most of their vitamins. Salt them just before serving (if you must use salt at all). For the same reason, cut them up just before you cook them.

Cooking garlic excessively makes it bitter. Just brown it—the lighter the color, the sweeter the flavor.

You can preserve certain seasonings in oil or vinegar. I like fresh dill very much, but cannot carry the plants when I travel, so I soak some in light oil and use it when I want the flavor to be real. Remember that preserved and frozen seasonings are more concentrated than fresh, so use less of them.

Hard-boiled (actually, long-simmered) eggs are a problem for many. To prevent cracking, take them out of the refrigerator half an hour ahead of time and stick a pin in the rounded end. Another way is to add salt, lemon juice, or vinegar to the water; this will keep the egg from coming out even if the shell does crack. If you have trouble peeling them, cook the eggs for 3 to 5 minutes, crack the shells all around with a knife handle, and cook for another 10 minutes. Take them out of the water and run cold water on them as you peel them.

Learn to know your oven's hot spots and cold spots. Take five slices of bread and place them on the middle rack, in all four corners and one in the center. Set the temperature at 400° and toast the slices, checking every so often to see which one becomes brown first and which reaches that stage last.

Saffron is one of the most expensive seasonings you could ever have occasion to buy. Would you believe it costs more than $2,000 a pound ($2,064)? If you want to make a dish that calls for it, buy a small container (0.007 ounce). The recipe will usually call for water, such as: "Cook the rice in 3 cups water flavored with saffron." Okay—add chicken base* to the water and *one eighth* the amount of saffron called for. You will be surprised—as I was—to find that the flavor actually carries

* From L. J. Minor Corp.—see page 31.

through the dish just as though you had put in the whole amount of saffron.

Here is a remarkable trick that works like a charm. You could cook vegetables in water, then sauté them in butter or oil and add seasonings— or simply put water in the bottom of a steamer, along with white wine, lemon juice, pepper, and the seasonings you want to incorporate into the vegetable. Let's assume that you are cooking carrots and cauliflower. Cut up the carrots and add fresh dill to the liquid in the steamer. When the carrots are almost done, add the cauliflower florets and finish them off. You can season any vegetable with any flavor just by adding the seasonings and herbs to the steaming water.

Keep in Mind...

Throughout the recipes, unless otherwise indicated:

"Butter" means unsalted butter.

"Pepper" means fresh ground black pepper; use white pepper for light-colored sauces and dishes.

"Flour" means all-purpose unbleached white flour. For baking, sift it before measuring, then sift it together with the other dry ingredients to disperse them evenly.

Potatoes, apples, etc., need not be peeled unless you like to peel them.

Generally, 1 tablespoon fresh herb equals 1 teaspoon dried herb.

Use pasteurized heavy cream, not ultrapasteurized, which has a cooked flavor and does not whip successfully.

Eggs are large.

Recommended seasonings such as Paul Prudhomme's Seafood Magic Seasoning, Creole mustard, and hoisin sauce are available in "gourmet" or ethnic food sections of many supermarkets. If you use prepared horseradish, read the label and buy a brand free from preservatives and other chemicals.

To grease a pan for baking, use butter or margarine, not oil.

Always preheat the oven to the desired temperature; many dishes need that initial blast of hot air to come out properly.

To make a roux, melt butter and in it cook an equal amount of flour over low heat for 4 to 6 minutes.

To prepare a mirepoix, cut celery, carrots, and onions into 1/2-inch dice.

Canned tomatoes come in a bewildering variety of sizes. Buy the size closest to what is called for in a recipe.

Feel free to multiply or divide recipes according to how many you have to feed.

THE BLACK HAT CHEF COOKBOOK

Appetizers and First Courses

*M*any of us wish to make an impression on guests whom we invite home for a classical dinner, so we try to serve something completely different and out of the ordinary. Hors d'oeuvres and canapés do that for us, but many are too well known. Here are a few that you can do quite easily, yet are different and impressive. Plan to serve more per person as a first course than as an appetizer.

STUFFED CHERRY TOMATOES

- 24 cherry tomatoes
- 1 1/2 tablespoons minced shallots
- 3 tablespoons sour cream
- 4 tablespoons chopped pecans
- 3 tablespoons minced celery
- 8 ounces cream cheese
- 1 tablespoon French brandy
- White pepper
- 24 parsley sprigs

Dig out the inside of each tomato to make a well for the filling. Mix all of the other ingredients, except the parsley, and fill the tomatoes with the mixture. Chill them for as long as you wish. When ready to serve, place a small sprig of parsley in the center of the filling and put the tomatoes on a serving platter.

Serves 10 to 12

EGGVIAR

- 4 eggs
- 1 jar black caviar (beluga)

Purchase a syringe that has a needle at least 1/8 inch in diameter. With an electric drill, drill a hole just a bit larger than the syringe tip size in the top of each raw egg. Insert the syringe into the egg; withdraw part of the albumen and discard it. Fill the syringe with caviar and insert it into the egg. Tape the hole with waterproof tape, then boil the eggs for at least 8 minutes, run cold water on them, and peel them right away. Slice the eggs and serve the slices on rounds of toast or Melba toast rounds.

Serves 8

This one will flip their wig. It is difficult, I know, but so well worth the effort that you will be envied for your talent.

STUFFED EGGS

- 8 eggs
- 2 large tablespoons prepared horseradish
- 4 ounces ham
- 3 tablespoons mayonnaise
- 2 tablespoons semisweet white wine
- Salt
- White pepper

Hard-boil the eggs and chill them. Cut them in half lengthwise. Remove the yolk and mix it with the other ingredients. Using a pastry tube with a star tip, fill the egg cavities. You can sprinkle on paprika or finely chopped parsley, if you like.

Serves 8

RAW VEGETABLE DIP

- 1/2 pint heavy cream, whipped
- 4 ounces cream cheese
- 2 tablespoons French brandy
- 1 garlic clove, finely minced
- 6 tablespoons finely chopped fresh parsley
- 1/4 cup sour cream
- 4 ounces plain yogurt
- 1 small onion, minced
- White pepper

Blend all of the ingredients in a food processor. Chill well and serve on a platter, surrounded by raw cauliflower, broccoli, celery sticks, carrot sticks, and so on.

Serves 10 to 12

People have come to realize that raw vegetables, served properly, are better for them than cooked. Try this dip to add variety.

CURRIED KING CRAB MEAT

8 ounces cream cheese
1 garlic clove, minced
1 tablespoon *hot* curry powder
Salt
Pepper
2 tablespoons heavy cream
2 teaspoons minced onion
2 tablespoons chopped fresh parsley
12 ounces crab meat, chopped into small pieces

Mix all of the ingredients until quite well blended. Spread the mixture on pieces of bread cut to any shape you like—stars, rounds, rectangles, or the like. Bake in the oven at 325° for about 15 minutes. Serve hot or cold.

Serves 10 to 12

PUFF PASTRY TARTILLANS

1 8-ounce package frozen spinach
1 tablespoon minced onion
4 hard-boiled eggs
4 tablespoons grated cheddar cheese
24 4-inch squares of puff pastry (page 183)
Melted butter

Purée the spinach, onion, eggs, and cheese. Set aside. Brush the pastry squares on the bottom with melted butter, place them on a cookie sheet, and brush the tops with water. Place a spoonful of the filling in the center of each square. Pull the opposite corners together, and try to pinch the four corners together to form a bundle. Bake in a preheated 400° oven until you see the pastry turn a rich golden brown. Serve hot or cold, as you prefer.

Serves 10 to 12

CHEESY CANAPÉS

- 96 slices cheese (any kind)
- 96 toasted bread pieces
- 1 small jar red caviar
- 1 small jar black caviar
- 12 slices pepperoni
- 4 hard-boiled eggs, grated
- 12 slices green olives
- 12 slices black olives
- 12 small cooked shrimp, peeled and deveined
- 4 large radishes, sliced
- 4 small slices of a good ham
- 12 slices chicken

Place the cheese on the bread. Heat them in a 400° oven, 12 at a time, to soften and melt the cheese. Then top each piece with any combination of the toppings in the ingredients. For example, place a shrimp and a sprinkling of grated egg on one. On another place a slice of ham, to fit the shape of the canapé, and on it a slice of olive. For still another, use a piece of chicken with a slice of radish. It is that easy; just use your imagination.

Makes 96

Canapés are an appetizer that can be served with delight if you do something different with them.

First, you should know what to serve them on and how to prepare what you will be using. Bread should almost always be used; get a firm type that will stand up to toasting or frying. A good bakery can provide it for you. Just tell them what you intend, and they can sell you the right product.

Second, purchase a set of cookie cutters in different shapes. Use these to cut out the canapé bases. Butter the cut bread-figures and bake them in a 360° oven for 15 minutes or more. When they turn brown, take them out and remove them from the pan right away. You could fry them in a skillet if you wished, but the oven method is better.

OYSTER CANAPÉS

- 18 shucked oysters, with their liquor
- 1/4 cup hollandaise sauce (page 245)
- Butter
- 12 1 1/2-inch bread rounds
- 2 tablespoons minced fresh parsley

Put the oysters and their liquor in a skillet or saucepan and cook over low heat just until they seem plump and the edges ruffle up. Drain the oysters and chop them. Combine with the hollandaise sauce. Butter the bread rounds on one side and sauté them in a pan until they are just browned on that side only. Mound the oyster mixture on the uncooked side and sprinkle with parsley. Gently press the parsley into the oyster mixture so that it adheres. Dot each canapé with a dab of butter. Place on a baking sheet and heat through in a preheated 375° oven. Serve 3 per person.

Serves 4

THE BATTER OF BATTERS—WITH BEER

- 2 cups flour
- Large pinch of salt
- 2 tablespoons baking powder
- 1 can or more flat beer

Mix the flour, salt, and baking powder; then mix the beer in slowly until the batter becomes semithick. Dip what you wish to serve—shrimp, oysters, clams, fish, or the like—in the batter. Cook in deep fat heated to 400° to 425°.

Serves 12

A very old and dear friend and mentor, chef Albert Stockli, from the Stonehenge Inn in Connecticut, taught me this beer batter for canapés, one of the best I have ever tried.

OYSTERS MOSCA

- Italian bread crumbs
- Olive oil
- 1 quart shucked oysters, with their liquor
- Fresh garlic juice (from a press)
- Rosemary
- Minced garlic
- Oregano
- Crushed whole peppercorns
- Chopped or ground bacon

Place a coating of bread crumbs on the bottom of a baking pan large enough to hold the oysters, and moisten it with olive oil. Lay the oysters on top and add their liquor, along with the seasonings. Place another coating of bread crumbs over the entire pan and sprinkle with oil. Then place a modest portion of bacon on top. Bake at 400° until golden brown.

Serves 24

Mr. Mosca taught me this himself, at L'Enfant's Restaurant in New Orleans.

OYSTERS BIENVILLE

- 4 tablespoons butter
- 8 shallots
- 2 tablespoons flour
- 1 cup chicken stock
- 1 cup chopped cooked small shrimp
- 8 ounces mushrooms, finely chopped
- 2 egg yolks
- 1/2 cup dry white wine
- 12 oysters, opened and left in the bottom shell
- 1/2 cup bread crumbs
- 2 tablespoons grated Parmesan cheese
- Paprika
- Salt
- Pepper

Melt the butter in a large saucepan. Finely chop the shallots and sauté them in the butter. Add the flour and make a roux by cooking it for about 5 minutes over a low flame. Add the chicken stock, shrimp, and mushrooms. Cook briefly. Beat together the egg yolks and wine and add to the saucepan. Cook until slightly thickened. Top each oyster with the mixture. Combine the bread crumbs, Parmesan, and a little paprika, salt, and pepper, and sprinkle over the sauce. Bake in a preheated 375° oven until it shows a slight browning on top. Serve 3 per person, with a slice of lemon on the side.

Serves 8

OYSTERS ROCKEFELLER

- 1/3 cup butter
- 1 1/4 cups frozen chopped spinach, thawed
- Large pinch of nutmeg
- 3 to 4 tablespoons minced onion
- 1/2 teaspoon salt
- 1/2 teaspoon white pepper
- 3/4 cup bread crumbs
- 1 jigger Pernod
- 12 oysters, opened and left in the bottom shell

Melt the butter in a large saucepan and add all of the remaining ingredients, except the oysters. Cook briefly and place on top of the oysters in the bottom shell. Bake in a preheated 375° oven until somewhat dry on top. Serve 3 per person, with a lemon wedge on the side.

Serves 6

BAKED OYSTERS WITH FINES HERBES

- 1 1/2 sticks (3/4 cup) butter
- 9 shallots, grated
- 1/4 cup minced fresh parsley
- 1/4 cup minced chives
- 1/4 cup cracker crumbs
- 2 teaspoons lemon juice
- Salt
- Pepper
- 36 oysters on the half shell

Make a paste with all of the ingredients, except the oysters. Line a small baking sheet pan with rock salt. Cover the oysters with the paste and set on the rock salt. Bake in a preheated 400°

oven for approximately 10 minutes, until the oysters are plump.

Serves 6

A favorite from the collection of my Associate Chef Danny McDole, on my TV series.

STUFFED CLAMS OR OYSTERS

- 18 cherrystone clams or oysters
- 4 tablespoons lemon juice
- 2 cups bread crumbs or cracker crumbs
- 2 tablespoons dry white wine
- 1/2 tablespoon crushed red pepper
- Just a bit of salt

Remove the clams or oysters from their shells. Chop them into small pieces. Mix the lemon juice, bread crumbs, wine, pepper, and salt. Add the chopped clams or oysters. Fill the shells with this mixture and bake at 400° until the top becomes crusty. Serve 3 per person, with a lemon wedge on the side.

Serves 6

CRAB MEAT SHIMODA

- 1 celery stalk
- 1 onion, minced
- 1/2 pint heavy cream
- 1/2 pint sour cream
- 1/2 pint plain yogurt
- 1/4 cup mayonnaise
- 7 to 8 tablespoons dry white wine
- 2 tablespoons lemon juice
- 2 large pinches of minced fresh dill
- Several pinches of Paul Prudhomme's Seafood Magic Seasoning
- 12 to 18 ounces crab meat
- Lettuce leaves

Very finely grind the celery and onion in a food processor or a blender. Whip the cream until thick. Add the sour cream and whip again. Add the yogurt and mayonnaise and whip again. Mix in the celery, onion, wine, lemon juice, dill, and seafood seasoning. Put a lettuce leaf on each appetizer dish. Place a generous amount of the sauce on it, and 2 to 3 ounces of crab meat.

Serves 6

I developed this dish for the Delta Point River Restaurant in Vicksburg, Mississippi. The Automobile Association of America awarded the restaurant four stars a mere thirteen days after it opened.

CRAB MEAT STUFFING FOR MUSHROOMS, SHRIMP, OR FISH

- 12 large club crackers
- 8 tablespoons melted butter (1 stick)
- 1/4 tablespoon crushed red pepper
- Juice of 1/2 lemon
- 4 ounces king crab meat, chopped
- 4 tablespoons chopped fresh parsley
- 4 tablespoons sauterne

- 12 large mushrooms, or 12 large shrimp, or 6 flounder or sole fillets

Crush the crackers to a semifine grind. Add the next six ingredients and mix to a soft, pasty consistency.

To stuff mushrooms, remove the stems, mound the stuffing in the caps, place in a buttered pie tin, and bake in a preheated 400° oven for 12 to 15 minutes. For shrimp, peel them, leaving on the tails, devein them, and stuff; bake in a buttered pie tin in a preheated 400° oven for 12 to 15 minutes. For fish, spread the stuffing on the skin side of the fillets and roll up. Place them on a buttered pie tin, rub them with butter and lemon juice, and bake in a preheated 375° oven for 20 minutes.

Serves 4 to 6

SNAILS IN MUSHROOMS

- 16 small mushroom caps
- 2 sticks (1 cup) butter
- 6 tablespoons finely minced garlic
- 4 tablespoons chopped fresh parsley
- 2 tablespoons dry white wine
- 16 snails

Clean the mushroom caps and set them in a baking dish. Soften the butter and mix it with the garlic, parsley, and wine. Place some of the mixture in the mushroom caps, top each with a snail, and generously cover the snail with more of the mixture. Bake at 400° until the mushrooms are cooked, 4 to 6 minutes or even more, if needed, until the mixture is completely melted. Serve 4 per person.

Serves 4

SHRIMP COCKTAIL

- 1/2 bottle ketchup
- 2 tablespoons lemon juice
- 5 to 6 tablespoons hot prepared horseradish
- 4 large lettuce leaves
- 16 medium-size shrimp, peeled, deveined, and cooked

Mix the ketchup, lemon juice, and horseradish. Make it as hot as you like. Place a lettuce leaf, whole or chopped into small pieces, in each serving dish and top it with sauce. Arrange 4 shrimp either on the lettuce or around the edge of it.

Serves 4

Most people have the impression that a good shrimp cocktail sauce has to have Worcestershire sauce, Tabasco sauce, onion, and chili sauce in it to make it right. Wrong. *Try this one. You will be surprised at how easy it is—and economical.*

SHRIMP RÉMOULADE

- 16 medium-size shrimp, peeled and deveined
- 2 tablespoons olive oil
- 1 tablespoon cider vinegar
- 1/2 teaspoon paprika
- White pepper
- 1 tablespoon prepared hot mustard (Creole type, if possible)
- 1/2 teaspoon drained prepared horseradish
- 1/2 celery stalk, very finely chopped
- 1 teaspoon grated onion
- 1 teaspoon minced fresh parsley
- Salt
- Salad greens

Put the shrimp in a pot of cold water with a bit of salt added. Bring to a boil, then turn off the heat and let the shrimp sit in the water for a few minutes. Drain and let cool. Combine all of the remaining ingredients, except the salt and greens. Season the sauce with salt, a bit at a time. Refrigerate the sauce for at least an hour. Make a bed of crisp greens on each serving plate. Put 4 shrimp on each and cover with sauce.

Serves 4

SHRIMP AND CUCUMBER SALAD

Vinegar Dressing

- 4 tablespoons rice wine vinegar
- 1/2 teaspoon salt
- 4 teaspoons sugar
- 2 teaspoons dark soy sauce

- 16 shrimp, peeled and deveined
- 2 small cucumbers
- 1 teaspoon salt
- 2 tablespoons sesame seeds

Mix the dressing ingredients and shake well to blend. Cook the shrimp, cut into bite-size pieces, and chill well. Peel and seed the cucumbers and cut them into very thin slices. Sprinkle them with salt and marinate for at least an hour. Mix the shrimp and cucumbers and toss with the dressing. Sprinkle with sesame seeds and serve in small appetizer dishes.

Serves 4

Note: Some prefer to roast the sesame seeds. I do not, but the choice is yours.

SQUID IN TOMATO SAUCE

- 1 pound squid
- 4 tablespoons olive oil
- 2 garlic cloves
- Salt
- Pepper
- Large pinch of oregano
- 1/2 cup dry sherry
- 1 cup solid-pack tomatoes
- 1 teaspoon chopped fresh parsley

Clean the squid and cut into small ringlike pieces. Heat the olive oil in a saucepan and brown the garlic in it for about 2 to 3 minutes; do not let it burn. Add the squid, cover, and cook for 10 minutes. Turn the heat off for a few minutes, then turn it on again and add the salt, pepper, oregano, and sherry. Cook for another 10 minutes. Turn the heat off again for a few minutes. Turn the heat back on, add the tomatoes and parsley, and cook for another 15 minutes. Serve very hot, on toast.

Serves 4

Note: Squid is very chewy—it can even be called tough. However, turning the heat off between each cooking step lets it marinate in its juices, tenderizing it. Do all the cooking over low heat.

FRIED SQUID

- 1 1/2 pounds very small squid
- 1/2 cup olive oil
- 1 large garlic clove
- 1 cup tomato sauce
- 1/2 cup dry white wine
- 1/2 teaspoon salt
- 1/8 teaspoon dried ground red pepper

Clean the squid and wash it thoroughly. Heat the oil in a preheated saucepan. Brown the garlic and discard it. Cook the squid over low to medium heat for 10 minutes. Turn the heat off for a few minutes. Add the tomato sauce, wine, salt, and pepper. Cover and cook for 15 minutes. Serve with a loaf of French or Italian bread on the side.

Serves 4

MARINATED CRAB CLAWS

- 16 crab claws
- 1/4 cup red wine vinegar
- 1/2 teaspoon tarragon leaves
- 1/2 cup minced green pepper
- 1/2 cup minced celery
- 1/2 cup minced scallions
- 1/2 teaspoon black pepper
- 1/2 cup olive oil
- 2 tablespoons lemon juice
- 5 garlic cloves, finely minced
- 1/2 cup finely chopped fresh parsley
- 1/4 teaspoon salt
- 1/4 teaspoon sugar
- 4 tablespoons dry vermouth

If the crab claws are purchased already cooked, just crack them, remove half of the shells, and set the claws in the refrigerator. If they are raw, steam them lightly and set aside to cool. Mix all of the remaining ingredients and refrigerate. When ready to serve, place the claws in a large serving bowl and cover with the marinade. Use a slotted spoon to pick up the claws. Serve with small French bread rolls on the side.

Serves 4

CRAWFISH ÉTOUFFÉE

- 2 sticks (1 cup) butter
- 1/2 cup flour
- 2 cups chopped onions
- 1/4 cup chopped celery
- 1/4 cup chopped green pepper
- 1/2 tablespoon minced garlic

- 16 crawfish tails
- 1/2 teaspoon salt
- 1 teaspoon black pepper
- 1/2 teaspoon cayenne pepper
- 1/8 teaspoon crushed red pepper
- 1 large pinch of cumin
- 1/4 cup chopped scallions, white part only, or 1/4 cup chopped shallots
- 1/2 tablespoon lemon juice
- 1/2 tablespoon minced fresh parsley
- 1/2 cup cold water

In a heavy 4- to 5-quart kettle over low heat, melt the butter. Gradually add the flour, and cook over low heat until it reaches a medium brown color. Cook slowly and stir almost continuously, to avoid burning. Add the onions, celery, green pepper, and garlic and cook, stirring often, until the vegetables are done, 15 to 20 minutes. Add the crawfish tails, salt, black pepper, cayenne, red pepper, cumin, scallions, lemon juice, and parsley. Add the cold water and bring to a boil; then lower the heat and simmer for 25 to 30 minutes.

Serves 6

Really Cajun! This dish can be served in many ways. Cajuns love it on rice. I like to serve it on squares of puff pastry or several layers of Greek phyllo pastry. I cut 4-inch squares of phyllo, butter them, and bake at 400° for about 12 minutes. Once it has reached a nice golden brown, it is done. Just spoon 4 of the crawfish tails with some of the sauce onto rice or pastry—and enjoy!

STUFFED BONELESS CHICKEN WINGS

- 12 middle sections of chicken wings
- 12 strips green peppers
- 12 slices Chinese mushrooms
- 12 slices water chestnuts
- 2 tablespoons hoisin sauce
- 4 tablespoons sake
- 1/2 cup coconut milk
- 1 tablespoon lemon juice

Cut the end of the bone from the middle section of each chicken wing. Push out the bone and stuff one piece of pepper, mushroom, and water chestnut into the cavity. Make a marinade of the hoisin sauce, sake, coconut milk, and lemon juice. Soak the chicken pieces in this for 30 to 60 minutes, then cook them in it. Serve 3 per person.

Serves 4

POP-A-CORNY CHICKEN

Mild cheese
Leftover cooked chicken
Popped popcorn, ground up

Melt the cheese over low heat. Cut the chicken into pieces, dip them in the cheese, and roll in the popcorn. Serve on long toothpicks.

Note: In a pinch, you could use Cheez Whiz and Cheez Doodles.

Short of putting a piece of cheese on a cracker, they don't come much easier than this. It's good, too.

CUBED CHICKEN WRAPPED IN SMOKED SALMON OR PROSCIUTTO

Marinade

- 2 tablespoons hoisin sauce
- 1 cup sake
- 1 tablespoon grated ginger root
- 4 tablespoons light brown sugar
- 2 tablespoons dark soy sauce
- 1/2 onion, grated
- 4 tablespoons oyster sauce

- 2 chicken breasts, boned and cut into 1-inch cubes
- 6 tablespoons sesame oil
- 1 piece smoked salmon or prosciutto per cube of chicken

Combine the marinade ingredients. Marinate the chicken for 4 hours. Heat the sesame oil in a pan and sauté the chicken until just done. Wrap each cube with salmon or prosciutto and secure with a toothpick.

Serves 4

CHICKEN LIVER PÂTÉ

- 1 small onion, chopped
- 4 tablespoons butter
- 16 chicken livers
- Juices of 2 lemons
- 16 tablespoons sauterne
- 16 slices bacon, cooked and crumbled
- 4 hard-boiled eggs

Sauté the onion in butter until translucent. Add the livers and cook for 4 to 5 minutes. Add the lemon juice and wine. Reduce the heat and cook until dry. Put the livers, bacon, and eggs in a food processor or blender and mix until smooth. Mound the mixture on a plate and chill before serving.

Serves 4

RUMAKI, JAPANESE STYLE

- 16 chicken livers
- 16 bamboo shoots or water chestnuts
- 8 slices bacon, blanched and cut in half
- 2 tablespoons hoisin sauce
- 4 tablespoons oyster sauce
- 4 tablespoons sake
- 1/2 tablespoon dark soy sauce
- 2 tablespoons dark brown sugar

Wrap a slice of chicken liver (or a whole liver, if you prefer) and a piece of bamboo shoot or water chestnut in a half slice of bacon. Marinate in a mixture of hoisin sauce, oyster sauce, sake, and soy sauce, and sugar. Bake in a preheated 350° oven until the bacon becomes slightly crisp. Turn once. Use the marinade to keep them slightly moist when baking. Make a duk sauce out of the rest of the marinade with the addition of a little oyster sauce.

Serves 4

SWISS FONDUE

- 1 pound Swiss cheese
- 2 tablespoons arrowroot powder
- Butter
- 2 garlic cloves, minced
- 1 1/2 cups dry white wine
- 1/2 cup semidry white wine
- 1 teaspoon lemon juice
- 1/16 teaspoon grated nutmeg
- White pepper
- 1/4 cup kirsch

Chop the cheese into small pieces; sprinkle the arrowroot over it and let it sit. Put the fondue pot over low heat. Melt a bit of butter in it and sauté the garlic. Take out the garlic and throw it away. Put the wines in the pot and heat slightly. Add the lemon juice. Using a wooden spoon, stir in the cheese, a bit at a time, melting each amount before adding more. Turn the heat up just a bit; as soon as the cheese is all melted and begins to bubble, add the nutmeg and pepper, then the kirsch. Serve it in the pot with fondue forks, and use chunks of French or Italian bread for dipping.

Serves 12 or more

Variations: Hot Pepper Fondue. Substitute a pound of hot pepper cheese for the Swiss cheese.

Cheesy Double Fondue. Use 1/2 pound each Gruyère and caraway cheese instead of the Swiss cheese.

PEAR WRAPPED IN HOT ITALIAN HAM

- 2 ripe pears
- 8 slices prosciutto or other spicy Italian ham
- 1 large container pear-flavored yogurt

Peel the pears. Core them and cut into quarters. Wrap each quarter with a slice of ham. Spread a layer of the yogurt on the bottom of each serving plate and place a pear quarter on top. Serves 4

Note: If you are going to prepare the pears quite some time ahead, leave the quartered pears in a pint of water mixed with the juice of half a lemon until you are ready to use them. This will keep the pears from turning color.

ASPARACADO WHEELS

- 4 slices white bread
- 8 short-stemmed asparagus spears
- 1 large avocado
- 1/4 cup mayonnaise
- Juice of 1/4 lemon
- 1 tablespoon white wine
- 1/2 teaspoon caraway seeds
- Salt
- White pepper

Trim off the bread crusts. Lay the slices out on a board and roll them flat with a rolling pin, but not so thin as to tear them. Steam the asparagus, then let cool. Peel the avocado and remove the pit. Cut the avocado into medium-thin slices. Mix the mayonnaise, lemon juice, wine, caraway seeds, and salt and pepper to taste. Spread this mixture on the bread. Place an asparagus spear at each end, the stem in the middle. Place avocado slices on the asparagus spears. Roll up and chill. To serve, cut into 1/2- to 1-inch slices.

Serves 4

FRIED CHEESE

- 12 strips firm cheese (such as mozzarella), each 3/4 inch wide and 4 to 5 inches long
- 1 cup flour
- 2 eggs, beaten well
- Italian seasoned bread crumbs
- Oil

Roll the cheese in flour; dip in the eggs and then the bread crumbs. Fry in at least 1 inch of oil in a large skillet until golden brown. Serve 3 per person. A nice dry wine goes well with this.

Serves 4

If you like, you can do this with zucchini sticks as well.

DOLMATHES

- 24 fresh grapevine leaves
- 1 pound lamb, finely chopped
- 1/2 cup raw rice, washed and dried
- 1 medium onion, finely grated
- 3 to 4 tablespoons pine nuts
- 4 tablespoons creamed corn
- 2 tablespoons fresh dill
- 4 tablespoons chopped fresh parsley
- Salt
- Pepper

Egg-Lemon Sauce

- 2 eggs
- 6 tablespoons lemon juice
- 1 teaspoon arrowroot powder

Blanch the leaves in boiling water for 1 to 2 minutes. Drain them and set aside. Mix the lamb, rice, onion, pine nuts, corn, dill, parsley, salt, and pepper. Line the bottom and sides of a buttered large pan with a few of the leaves. Trim the stalk off the remaining leaves and fill each from the large end with stuffing; fold the stem over, tuck in the sides, and roll into a shape resembling a large sausage. Place the end of the leaf underneath and lay an object of some sort on the top of them to hold them together. Pour 1 to 2 pints hot water over them. Cover the pan, place in a 375° oven, and bake for about 1 hour.

Remove from the oven and drain the liquid carefully from the pan. Beat the eggs with the lemon juice. Add the arrowroot, mixed with a bit of warm water, and beat well. Pour over the stuffed grape leaves and put the pan on the stove over low heat; simmer for about 5 minutes, but do not let it come to a boil at any time. Once the leaves have incorporated the sauce, you can serve them, 4 per person.

Serves 6

CAPONATA

- 4 tablespoons olive oil
- 1 eggplant, with the skin left on, cut into small cubes
- 1 finely chopped onion
- 2 garlic cloves, finely chopped
- 2 tablespoons minced fennel (*not* fennel seeds)
- 1/2 cup chopped celery
- 1/2 cup chopped green and black olives
- 1/2 cup chopped tomatoes
- 1/8 teaspoon sugar
- 2 tablespoons red wine vinegar
- 2 tablespoons capers
- Salt
- Black pepper

*H*eat the oil in a large skillet. Add the eggplant and sauté to a light golden color. Remove from the skillet and drain well. Sauté the onion, garlic, fennel, and celery, and add the remaining ingredients. Cook until the celery is soft. Add the eggplant and cook until it is rather soft. Serve chilled or just cooled, with garlic bread or regular Italian bread.

Serves 4

QUESO

- 4 tablespoons oil
- 1 yellow onion, finely chopped
- 1/2 cup finely chopped green pepper
- 1/2 pound thinly sliced mushrooms
- 1 pound Monterey Jack cheese
- 1/2 cup heavy cream
- 8 flour or corn tortillas, toasted

Heat oil in a large skillet. Sauté the onion and pepper. Add the mushrooms and cook until done. In a double boiler, melt the cheese slowly. Mix in the cream. Add the mushroom mixture and blend well. Spoon the mixture onto the tortillas and serve, 2 per person.

Serves 4

SOUPS

*T*here is so much to be said for soups—they can be served with classical dinners, for guests on special occasions, or just for plain meals.

No matter what kind of soups you make, *no* soup that has cream or any type of pasta in it can be frozen. The reason is quite simple: cream curdles when thawed, and pasta turns to mush. Nor should fruit soups be frozen. Also, most soups should not be kept for more than two or three days, refrigerated.

I have listed servings per recipe, but this can vary greatly, depending on whether it is being served as a first course or a full one.

Cold Soups

COLD CREAM OF TOMATO SOUP

- 3 cups fresh tomatoes, cut into small pieces
- 1 small onion, coarsely chopped
- Small pinch of ground cloves
- 1/2 cup water
- 3 tablespoons flour
- 3 tablespoons butter
- 3 cups cream or half-and-half
- Salt
- White pepper
- Chopped fresh parsley

Put the tomatoes, onion, cloves, and water in a large pot and bring to a boil. Simmer for at least 20 minutes. Remove to a food processor, purée it, and set it aside. Make a roux by cooking the flour in the butter for about 6 to 8 minutes over a low flame. Do not let it get dark. When it is done, begin adding the cream, a bit at a time, until it becomes a rather thick cream sauce (a béchamel). Combine it with the tomato mixture and just heat through. Add salt and pepper to taste. Chill well, and serve with a large sprinkling of parsley on top.

Serves 6

COLD CHICKEN SOUP

- 3 large scallions
- Butter
- 4 cups chicken stock
- 1 cup light beer
- White pepper
- 12 to 16 ounces cooked chicken meat, cut into julienne 1/2 inch thick
- 6 slices hard-boiled egg

Chop the scallions into small pieces and place in a small pan. Add a small amount of butter, set in a 360° oven, and bake for about 10 minutes. Remove and set aside.

Heat the chicken stock and add the beer and pepper. Let it

simmer for 10 to 12 minutes, then add the chicken to heat through. Refrigerate until cooled, then remove the chicken strips. Add the scallions to the stock and purée the stock in a food processor or blender. Add the chicken to it again and check for seasoning. Serve in cold soup cups with egg slices for garnish.

Serves 6

This soup comes from Russia, where it is called okrushka.

CHILLED ALMOND SOUP

- 1/3 cup blanched almonds
- 2 scallions, white part only
- 1 small celery stalk
- 2 cups chicken stock
- 2 cups heavy cream
- Dash of mace
- Salt
- White pepper
- Chopped fresh parsley

Finely grind together the almonds, scallions, and celery. Heat the chicken stock and add the ground mixture. Simmer for at least a half hour. Force through a fine sieve, then add the cream and seasonings to taste, being careful not to add too much mace. Chill, and serve topped with parsley.

Serves 4

COLD EAST INDIAN SOUP

- 2 small onions, minced
- 1 tablespoon butter
- 1 garlic clove
- 1/2 teaspoon curry powder
- 1 tablespoon flour
- 1 quart chicken stock
- 1 sour green apple, cored and finely chopped
- 2 fresh tomatoes, chopped
- 2 tablespoons grated coconut
- 1 teaspoon lemon juice
- 1 pint heavy cream

Slightly brown the onions in the butter. Add the garlic, curry powder, and flour. Cook for several minutes. Add the chicken stock, apple, tomatoes, coconut, and lemon juice, and simmer, covered, for 2 hours. Strain and cool. Blend in the cream just before serving.

Serves 4

ROMANOFF'S SENEGALESE SOUP

- 4 cups chicken stock
- 2 tablespoons butter
- 1 1/2 tablespoons curry powder
- 2 egg yolks
- 1 cup heavy cream
- 1 small avocado, diced

Heat the chicken stock, add the butter and curry powder, and blend well. Beat the egg yolks, mix with the cream, and stir into the chicken stock. Simmer very slowly until it becomes somewhat thick. Chill well and garnish with avocado.

Serves 4

TANABOUN

- 2 onions, finely minced
- 2 celery stalks, finely minced
- 4 tablespoons melted butter
- 1 pint sour cream
- 2 cups clarified chicken stock
- 1 pint plain yogurt
- 2 jiggers semisweet white wine
- White pepper
- Paprika

Sauté the minced onion and celery in the butter until soft. Put all of the ingredients, except paprika, in a food processor or blender and purée them. Pour the purée into a pot, heat to a simmer, and let it simmer for 5 minutes. Remove from the pot, chill, and serve with a sprinkling of paprika on top.

Serves 6

BORSCHT

- 1 pint beef stock
- 1 pint canned tomatoes
- 1 large onion, minced
- 1 garlic clove, minced
- 2 16-ounce cans sliced beets
- 1 bay leaf
- 2 tablespoons sugar
- 1 tablespoon paprika
- 4 parsley sprigs
- 1/4 teaspoon salt
- Pepper
- 6 tablespoons sour cream

Put the stock, tomatoes, onion, and garlic in a pot and bring to a boil. When the onion is soft, add the remaining ingredients except sour cream, and simmer for 1 hour. Remove the bay leaf. Force the soup through a sieve, then chill it. Serve in chilled soup cups, with a large tablespoon of sour cream on top of each.

Serves 6

BORSCHT, POLISH STYLE

- 3/4 pound canned sliced beets
- 2 tablespoons chopped onion
- 1/2 cup vinegar
- 1 tablespoon sugar
- 1 1/2 pints water
- 1 tablespoon lemon juice
- Salt
- Pepper
- 2 tablespoons sour cream

Drain the beets. Put the beet juice, onion, vinegar, sugar, and 1 pint water in a large soup pot. Simmer until the onion is cooked. Chop or dice the beets. When the onion is done, add the rest of the water and the beets and lemon juice. Bring to a boil, then check for seasoning. Remove from the heat and let cool.

Serves 6

If you add the vinegar a bit at a time, the soup will come out just the way you like it. Do not follow this or any other recipe word for word and by the exact measurements; season a bit at a time to reach your own final taste-goal.

BORSCHT, RUSSIAN STYLE

- 1 1/2 quarts beef stock
- 1/2 cup canned tomatoes
- 2 tablespoons diced onion
- 1/8 teaspoon minced garlic
- 3/4 pound canned beets, with juice
- 1/4 cup lemon juice
- 2 tablespoons parsley sprigs
- 1 tablespoon sugar
- 1/4 teaspoon paprika
- 1/2 bay leaf
- 3/8 teaspoon salt
- Pepper
- Sour cream

Put the beef stock, tomatoes, onion, and garlic in a stockpot and simmer until the onion is done. Add the remaining ingredients, except sour cream, and simmer for 1 1/2 hours. Strain the soup through a large china cap, forcing through as much of the pulp as you can. Serve cold or hot, garnished with sour cream.

Serves 6

CHILLED PLUM SOUP

- 1 pound plums, pitted
- 6 tablespoons sugar
- Zest of 1/2 lemon
- 8 cups water
- 2 jiggers plum wine
- 5 whole cloves

Put all of the ingredients in a pot and bring to a boil. Turn the flame down and simmer until the fruit is very soft. Remove the lemon zest and cloves, purée the plums, and refrigerate the soup until chilled.

Serves 6 to 8

Serve this sweet soup garnished with a small lemon cookie or a piece of angel food cake.

MELON CREAM SOUP

- 2 large ripe honeydew melons (about 3 pounds each)
- 1 cup heavy cream
- 4 tablespoons port
- 4 teaspoons finely chopped mint
- 1 small cucumber, peeled, cut in half lengthwise, seeded, and very thinly sliced
- Mint sprigs

Cut the melons in half and scrape out the seeds and strings. Scoop out the flesh and purée it in a food processor or blender. Strain through a fine sieve into a large bowl. You should have about 6 cups. Add the cream, port, and chopped mint. Refrigerate, covered, for at least an hour before serving. In serving bowls or a tureen, float thin slices of cucumber on the soup, and garnish with mint sprigs.

Serves 6

COLD PEACH SOUP

- 5 large ripe peaches, peeled and quartered
- 3 to 4 tablespoons sugar
- 1/4 cup sour cream
- 1/4 cup fresh lemon juice
- 1/4 cup sweet sherry
- 2 tablespoons thawed orange juice concentrate
- Fresh peaches, peeled and sliced

Purée the quartered peaches with sugar in a food processor or blender. Mix in the sour cream. Add the lemon juice, sherry, and orange juice, and blend until smooth. Transfer to a bowl, cover, and refrigerate until well chilled. Ladle the soup into bowls. Garnish each bowl with peach slices and serve.

Serves 6 to 8

Hot Soups

There are four ways to make stock: from the natural product itself (meat, chicken, etc.), from a good base, from liquid purchased in a can, and from a bouillon cube. There is never quite enough time for the average person to do it from scratch, so I suggest a base. The L. J. Minor Corp. of Cleveland, Ohio, sells excellent bases for soups and sauces; to order, call 1 (800) 441-5914. Purchase one for, say, chicken. Boil the amount of water for the amount of soup you wish to make (for two people, 1 quart). Add some of the base to the water, and keep tasting until it reaches the flavor you desire. You now have the stock for the soup. Do you wish to make a chicken rice soup? Fine—just add some chopped, diced, or even ground-up chicken and a bit of chopped or ground onion, carrot, and celery. (This is called a mirepoix, used to make the soup stock rich with an abundance of flavor.) Cook this in the stock, add cooked rice, season with salt and pepper, and you are done.

Once you have chicken stock you can make soups of many varieties. For example, buy broccoli or cauliflower. Cut off the stems, finely chop them, and sauté them in butter. Simmer the florets in a pot of chicken stock until soft. Add the sautéed stems and season to taste. *Voilà!*

But perhaps you want to make cream of broccoli soup. Make a béchamel: take cream, half-and-half, milk, or even skim milk, and thicken it with a roux. A roux is nothing more than equal parts of flour and butter cooked together over a medium to low flame for 5 to 10 minutes. (Stir it often to keep it from getting too dark.) Add the béchamel to the clear broccoli soup and you have cream of broccoli soup. It is as easy as that!

CHICKEN STOCK

- 1 5-pound chicken, cut up
- 2 carrots, peeled and chopped
- 2 celery stalks, chopped
- 1 onion, peeled and chopped
- 12 parsley sprigs

Put all of the ingredients in a pot and cover with water. Bring to a boil, then simmer for 2 hours. Skim the fat from the stock. Remove the chicken. (Use it for a garnish in chicken soup, or for chicken salad.) Strain the stock through cheesecloth and let cool.

Makes approximately 5 quarts

OSUIMONO SOUP

- 6 cups chicken stock
- 1 1/2 teaspoons light soy sauce
- 1 teaspoon sugar
- 1/2 teaspoon salt
- 1 1/2 cups diced cooked chicken
- 2 scallions, finely chopped
- 4 parsley sprigs

Combine the chicken stock, soy sauce, sugar, and salt and bring to a boil. Set on simmer, and mix in the chicken and scallions. Serve garnished with parsley sprigs.

Serves 4

FRENCH ONION SOUP

- 3 medium to large onions
- 8 tablespoons (1 stick) butter
- 2 cups chicken stock
- 2 cups beef stock
- 1 tablespoon each port and sherry
- Salt
- Pepper
- 5 slices French bread
- 5 slices mozzarella cheese

Cut each onion in half lengthwise. Cut across into slices about 1/8 inch thick. Sauté them in butter for a few minutes, then put a cover on the pot, lower the heat, and cook for 5 to 10 minutes. Uncover, add the stocks, and bring to a boil. Lower the heat and simmer for 5 minutes. Add the wines and seasoning and simmer for about 20 minutes.

Lightly butter the bread, cover with slices of cheese, and bake until slightly browned but not too crusty. Remove, let cool, and cut into bite-size pieces. Put about 12 to 14 pieces in each bowl and pour on the soup.

Serves 5

CREOLE-STYLE ONION SOUP

- 6 large onions
- 1 medium turnip
- 1/2 medium head white celery
- 8 tablespoons (1 stick) butter
- 3 cups boiling water
- 1/2 tablespoon anchovy paste or mashed fillets
- 1 blade mace
- 1/8 teaspoon allspice
- 1 1/2 cups soft bread crumbs
- Milk
- Salt
- Pepper
- 1 egg yolk
- Minced fresh parsley or croutons or sautéed slices of French bread

Chop the onions, turnip, and celery. Melt the butter in a large skillet and add the vegetables. Cook over moderate heat, stirring frequently, until golden brown. Do not let them burn. Turn them into a stockpot, along with any butter remaining in the pan. Add the boiling water, anchovy paste, mace, and allspice. Simmer until the vegetables are tender. Purée them together through a sieve. Return them to the stock (discarding the mace) and cook over low heat for 30 minutes. Moisten the bread crumbs with a little milk and mash to a paste. Add to the soup and blend. Correct the seasoning with salt and pepper (or more anchovy paste, if desired). Cook gently for 10 to 15 minutes.

Beat the egg yolk, and heat it by adding a spoonful of the hot soup. Pour the mixture slowly into the soup and blend. Cook for 3 to 4 minutes, stirring constantly. Serve with parsley, croutons, or bread slices.

Serves 4 to 5

VEGETABLE BEEF SOUP

- 1 pound lean beef, cut into 1/2-inch dice
- 1 cup mirepoix (chopped celery, carrots, and onions)
- 2 tablespoons oil
- 2 bay leaves
- 1 quart beef stock
- 1/2 cup diced potato
- 1 cup cooked mixed vegetables (may use leftovers)
- 1/2 cup chopped tomatoes
- Salt
- Pepper

Sauté the beef and mirepoix in oil. Add the bay leaves and beef stock and bring to boil. Add the potato and cook until done. Add the vegetables and tomatoes and heat through. Adjust the seasoning and serve.

Serves 4

POTAGE DUCHESSE

- 1/3 cup finely chopped carrots
- 3/8 cup finely chopped celery
- 2 teaspoons finely chopped onion
- 3 to 3 1/2 tablespoons butter
- 2 tablespoons flour
- 1 3/4 cups milk
- 1 3/4 cups chicken stock
- 5 ounces sharp cheddar cheese
- Chopped fresh parsley

Simmer the carrots and celery in 1 cup water until tender, about 15 minutes. Sauté the onion in butter until soft but not browned. Add the flour and blend well. Set the pan over hot water, add the milk and chicken stock, and cook until thickened, stirring constantly. Add the cheese and stir until blended. Add the cooked vegetables and their cooking water and heat thoroughly. Serve garnished with parsley.

Serves 5

RHODE ISLAND CLAM CHOWDER

- 2 large onions, cut into 1/2-inch dice
- 8 ounces salt pork, cut into 1/2-inch dice
- 3 large potatoes, peeled, blanched, and cut into 1/2-inch dice
- 6 large quahogs or 10 large clams, chopped
- 12 ounces clam juice
- Salt
- Pepper

Sauté the onions in salt pork until translucent. Bring 2 quarts water to a boil, then reduce the heat and simmer the potatoes, clams, and clam juice for 6 to 8 minutes. Season to taste and serve.

Serves 4; makes 2 quarts

Variation: New England Clam Chowder. Add cream or béchamel sauce; it should be served slightly thick.

MANHATTAN CLAM CHOWDER

- 1 quart Rhode Island clam chowder
- 1 celery stalk, cut into 1-inch dice
- 1 leek, cut into 1-inch dice
- 1/2 green pepper, seeded and cut into 1-inch dice
- 8 ounces canned tomatoes, (with juice), cut into 1-inch dice
- 1/2 tablespoon crushed garlic
- 1/2 teaspoon thyme
- 1/2 teaspoon rosemary
- Butter

Heat up the chowder. Sauté the vegetables and herbs. Add to the chowder, season to taste, and serve.

Serves 4

SEAFOOD GUMBO FILÉ

- 4 tablespoons butter
- 3 to 4 tablespoons flour
- 1 celery stalk, chopped
- 1 small onion, chopped
- 1 garlic clove, chopped
- 1 12-ounce can tomatoes
- 1 pound small shrimp, peeled and deveined
- 1/2 pound fish, flaked
- Salt
- Pepper
- 8 ounces frozen or canned okra, chopped
- 1/2 teaspoon filé

Make a roux with the butter and flour. When it is cooked, add the celery, onion, and garlic, and cook until tender. Add the tomatoes and 2 tomato cans of water. Add the shrimp and fish. Season to taste and simmer until done. Then add the okra. When you are ready to serve the soup, sprinkle filé on the bowl or cup of gumbo.

Serves 4

Note: If you use fresh okra, add it early enough so it can cook for 10 to 12 minutes.

A soup that is a meal in itself.

CHICKEN AND SHRIMP GUMBO FILÉ

- 1 4-pound chicken, cut into pieces
- 1 garlic clove
- Salt
- Pepper
- 1/4 pound salt pork, diced
- 1 sweet red pepper, seeded and cut up
- 1 cup chopped onions

- 1/2 cup flour
- 2 1/2 cups (1 1-pound 3-ounce can) tomatoes
- 1 10-ounce package frozen okra, thawed
- 1 pound shrimp, peeled and deveined
- Hot pepper sauce
- 2 teaspoons gumbo filé powder
- Hot cooked rice

Cook the chicken with 5 cups water, the garlic, 1 tablespoon salt, and 1/4 teaspoon pepper for 30 minutes, or until tender. Let cool and remove the meat from the bones; cut into pieces. Strain the stock, add enough water to make 6 cups, let cool, and skim off the fat. Cook the salt pork until well browned. Remove it from the kettle and pour off all but 1/4 cup fat. Sauté the red pepper and onions in the fat for 5 minutes. Add the flour and brown it. Gradually stir in the stock. Add the salt pork and tomatoes, cover, and simmer for 30 minutes. Add the chicken, okra, and shrimp. Simmer, covered, until the shrimp turn pink. Season with salt, pepper, and hot pepper sauce. Gradually add the filé powder, and stir until completely blended. Put a scoop of rice in each soup bowl and fill with gumbo filé.

Serves 6

CHICKEN AND OKRA GUMBO

- 1 3-pound frying chicken, cut up
- 2 tablespoons lard or butter
- 1 pound smoked ham, cut into 1/2-inch dice
- 1 onion, chopped
- 6 large fresh tomatoes, peeled and chopped
- 2 pints okra, sliced 1/2 inch thick
- Salt
- Cayenne pepper
- Few parsley sprigs, chopped
- 1 bay leaf
- 1 pod dried red pepper, without seeds
- 6 cups water
- 12 shucked oysters
- Hot cooked rice

Cut the chicken into 12 pieces. Heat lard in a heavy kettle. Add the chicken and ham. Cover and cook slowly for 10 minutes. Add the onion, tomatoes, and okra. Cook, stirring, over high heat for 4 to 5 minutes. Season with salt and cayenne. Add parsley, bay leaf, red pepper, and water. Bring to a boil, cover, and simmer for 1 1/2 to 2 hours. Add the oysters and cook for a few minutes. Add more salt and cayenne, if necessary. Serve with rice.

Serves 6 to 8

CREOLE BOUILLABAISSE

- 1 tablespoon butter
- Flour
- 1 onion, chopped
- 1 garlic clove, minced
- 1 teaspoon curry powder
- Dash of hot pepper sauce
- 4 whole cloves
- 1 bay leaf
- 1/4 teaspoon crumbled dried thyme
- 1/2 teaspoon salt
- 1 3/4 cups canned tomatoes
- 1/2 cup water
- 1 pound red snapper, cut into small pieces
- 1 pound redfish, cut into small pieces
- 1/4 cup sherry
- 2 ounces (1/2 4-ounce can) mushroom caps, undrained

Melt the butter in a skillet. Add the flour and cook over low heat until golden brown, stirring constantly. Add the onion and garlic; continue cooking for 2 to 3 minutes. Add the curry powder, hot pepper sauce, half of the cloves, half of the bay leaf, and the thyme and salt. After a minute or two, add the tomatoes and water. Simmer slowly, covered, for 30 minutes.

Put the fish in another skillet. Cover with boiling water; add the remaining cloves and bay leaf and half of the sherry. Lower the heat and simmer gently for 8 minutes; drain. Put the fish and mushrooms in the sauce and heat for 5 minutes. Add the remaining sherry and serve.

Serves 6

Cooking the seasonings in a roux gives this dish a very special flavor.

CRAB SOUP WITH TOMATOES AND GARLIC

- 4 or 5 hard-shell crabs, plus the meat from 5 more crabs
- 2 quarts water
- 2 tablespoons lard
- 1 large onion, chopped
- 4 garlic cloves, minced
- 1 rounded tablespoon flour
- 1 cup peeled and chopped tomatoes
- 1/4 teaspoon dried thyme
- 1 bay leaf
- Salt
- Pepper
- Cayenne pepper
- 2 egg yolks
- 1 rounded tablespoon butter
- Yolks of hard-boiled eggs

Boil the crabs in water to cover. When they are bright red, drain them and discard the water. Pick over the crab meat and reserve. Put the shells and all the trimmings (except the spongy lungs) in a heavy pot with the 2 quarts water. Bring to a boil and skim. Reduce the heat and simmer for 20 minutes. Strain and reserve the broth.

Melt the lard in a heavy soup kettle. Add the onion and garlic and cook over moderate heat until they are golden, stirring frequently. Add the flour, blend, and let brown. Add the tomatoes and herbs. Cook for 5 minutes, stirring from time to time. Add the reserved broth and the crab meat; reduce the heat to low and simmer for 1 hour. Season to taste with salt, pepper, and cayenne.

Just before serving, beat the raw egg yolks. Add 1 or 2 spoonfuls of the hot soup to them and blend, then slowly stir the mixture into the soup. Cook, stirring constantly, for 3 to 4 minutes. Stir in the butter, garnish with hard-boiled egg yolks, and serve.

Serves 6 to 8

CREAM OF CRAB SOUP

- Yolks of 2 hard-boiled eggs
- 4 tablespoons butter
- 1 tablespoon flour
- Grated zest of 1 lemon
- 1 teaspoon Worcestershire sauce
- 1 dash of hot pepper sauce or Tabasco sauce
- 1/8 teaspoon mace
- 1 shallot or scallion, minced
- 3 cups half-and-half
- 2 cups heavy cream
- 2 cups crab meat
- Salt
- White pepper
- Cayenne pepper
- 2 tablespoons Madeira or sherry, or to taste

Mash the egg yolks in a bowl and blend with 3 tablespoons of the butter and the flour, lemon zest, Worcestershire sauce, hot pepper sauce, and mace. Let stand while you sauté the shallot in the remaining 1 tablespoon butter over low heat. Do not brown it. Heat the half-and-half and cream together in the top of a large double boiler over hot water. Slowly stir in the egg mixture, shallot, and crab meat. Cook for 20 minutes, stirring frequently. Season to taste with salt, pepper, and cayenne. Add the wine just before serving.

Serves 6 to 8

SHRIMP BISQUE

- 2 cups shrimp stock
- 2 cups half-and-half
- 1/4 cup roux (equal parts flour and butter, cooked)
- 1/4 cup mirepoix (chopped celery, carrots, and onions)
- 8 ounces shrimp, peeled, deveined, and cubed
- 1 tablespoon butter
- 1/4 cup sherry
- Salt
- Pepper

Combine the shrimp stock and half-and-half; bring to a boil. Thicken with the roux and simmer in the top of a double boiler for 10 minutes. Sauté the mirepoix and shrimp in butter. Add the sherry and reduce by half. Combine the mirepoix and shrimp mixture with the soup. Season to taste, heat through, and serve. Bisques are thick, so add more roux if necessary.

Serves 4

CREAM OF TOMATO SOUP

- About 2/3 cup tomato juice
- 1 whole peppercorn
- 1/4 bay leaf
- 1 thin slice onion
- 1 tablespoon tomato paste
- 1 tablespoon butter
- 1 tablespoon flour
- 1/4 teaspoon salt
- 1/2 cup milk

Simmer together for 5 minutes the tomato juice, peppercorn, bay leaf, and onion, then strain into a glass measuring cup. Add enough tomato juice to bring the volume to 2/3 cup; add the tomato paste and blend.

Make a white sauce by melting the butter in a saucepan, adding flour and salt, and blending until smooth; add the milk gradually, off the heat, constantly stirring to form a smooth paste. Bring the mixture to a boil, stirring constantly. Add the tomato juice mixture and heat to serving temperature, but do not let it boil.

Serves 2

CHEDDAR CHEESE SOUP

- 1 quart chicken stock
- 1 quart half-and-half
- 1/2 cup roux (equal parts flour and butter, cooked)
- 1 pound cheddar cheese, grated
- Salt
- Pepper

Combine the chicken stock and half-and-half; bring to a boil. Thicken with the roux and simmer in the top of a double boiler for 10 minutes. Blend in the cheese. Adjust the seasoning and serve.

Serves 4

Variation: Peanut Butter Soup. Substitute peanut butter for the cheese.

DRIED PEA SOUP PAGO PAGO

- 2 ounces dried green peas
- 2 to 3 tablespoons orange juice
- 1/4 teaspoon ground mace
- 1 tablespoon grated orange zest
- 3/4 cup milk
- 2 cups water
- 1/2 cup popped popcorn

Combine all of the ingredients, except the popcorn, in a 2-quart saucepan and mix well. Cook, uncovered, over medium heat for 15 minutes, stirring occasionally. Serve at once, in mugs or soup bowls, and top with popcorn.

Serves 4

MEAT

Beef

BEEF WELLINGTON

- 4 6- to 8-ounce pieces of tenderloin
- 1 pound mushrooms, very finely chopped or grated
- Melted butter
- 2 medium onions or 8 shallots, chopped
- Salt
- Pepper
- Lemon juice
- 1/4 cup chopped fresh parsley
- 8 phyllo leaves
- 1 egg, beaten

Sauté the tenderloin and let cool. Wrap the mushrooms in a towel and squeeze out the excess liquid. Heat some butter in a saucepan and sauté the onions until lightly browned. Add the mushrooms, salt, pepper, and a few drops of lemon juice, and stir over high heat until all moisture has evaporated. Stir in the parsley and let cool.

Place a phyllo leaf on a damp cloth and brush with melted butter. Place a second leaf over the first. Place one tenderloin in the middle of the dough and spread the mushroom mixture over the top of the fillet. Fold a side of dough over half the fillet, and fold the opposite side over to meet it. Fold the remaining sides under, and brush the top with cold water. Repeat with the other fillets and phyllo. Place all on a cookie sheet, seams down. Brush with egg wash, and bake in a preheated oven at 375° for 15 to 20 minutes, or until golden.

Serves 4

Variation: Substitute pâté de foie gras for the mushroom mixture.

STUFFED TENDERLOIN

- 2 1/2 pounds center cut of beef tenderloin
- 1 cup thinly sliced green and red peppers
- 1/2 cup thinly sliced mushrooms
- 1/2 cup thinly sliced onion
- 2 tablespoons crushed peppercorns
- 2 pork sausages, blanched and sliced lengthwise
- Oil

Have the tenderloin cut to resemble a jelly roll or bracciole. On it place a layer of peppers, a layer of mushrooms, and a layer of onion. Sprinkle with peppercorns. Place the sausages on the mixture. Roll up the tenderloin as you would a jelly roll, and secure with toothpicks. Rub with oil and roast at 250° for 30 minutes for medium rare. Remove the toothpicks and slice. Serve on a Madeira brown sauce (page 247).

Serves 4 to 6

CARPETBAGGER

- 4 8-ounce tenderloin steaks
- 8 large oysters, shucked
- 4 slices bacon

Cut a pocket in each steak. Stuff 2 oysters into each pocket. Wrap each steak with bacon and secure with a toothpick. Broil for approximately 5 minutes on each side for medium rare and to crisp the bacon.

Serves 4

TOURNEDOS ROSSINI

- 4 9- to 10-ounce tenderloin fillets
- Demiglaze sauce (available from L. J. Minor Corp.)
- 2 tablespoons Madeira
- 4 slices goose liver
- 4 mushroom caps, trimmed (see note) and sautéed in butter

Slice the fillets in half and cook to order. Mix the demiglaze sauce and Madeira to the desired consistency. Put some of the sauce on each dinner plate. Place the tenderloin on the sauce, and put a slice of goose liver on each slice, topped with just a dab of sauce. Then top with a mushroom cap.

Serves 4

Note: Flute the mushroom caps decoratively: draw a knife at an angle from the top of the center of the mushroom to the bottom, slicing out a piece at an angle. If you want to get fancy, you can cut the initial of each guest on the top of the mushroom.

MEDALLIONS OF TENDERLOIN JOSEPH

- 4 8- to 10-ounce tenderloins
- Béarnaise sauce (page 246)
- Demiglaze sauce (available from L. J. Minor Corp.)
- 8 asparagus spears
- 4 cherry tomatoes

Slice the tenderloins in half. Cook to your preference. Place béarnaise sauce on half of the dinner plate, demiglaze sauce on the other half. Put one piece of meat on each of the sauces. Set 2 spears of asparagus and a cherry tomato in the very center of the plate.

Serves 4

Tenderloin is by far the most tender of all meats, but what do you do when you can't afford this cut? Did you know that you can make a piece of chuck almost as tender as tenderloin? Simply marinate it in papaya or pineapple juice for an hour or more—even overnight, if you have the time. Believe me, it will not alter the taste, and will be good for you as well. If you are unable to buy either of those two juices, use lemon juice, but rinse off the meat before you cook it.

MINI BOULAGE

Marinade

- 1 tablespoon sweet basil
- 1 tablespoon oregano
- 1/4 teaspoon each salt and pepper
- 1 cup olive oil
- 1 tablespoon Worcestershire sauce
- 1 tablespoon red wine vinegar
- 1/2 cup Burgundy

- 4 4-ounce tenderloin steaks
- 1 cup quartered mushrooms
- 1/2 cup quartered cherry tomatoes
- 1/2 cup sliced green peppers

Combine all the dry ingredients of the marinade. Add all the liquid ingredients and mix. Pour the marinade over the steaks and vegetables and marinate for 24 hours.

Bring the marinade and vegetables to a boil in a pan. Add the steaks and cook for 3 minutes on each side for medium rare. Remove the steaks to a platter and reduce the liquid. Pour the liquid and vegetables over the steaks.

Serves 4

PRIME RIB AU JUS

- 3- or 4-rib roast
- Salt
- Pepper
- Garlic powder

Mirepoix (chopped celery, carrots, and onions)
Beef base (optional; available from L. J. Minor Corp.)
Sherry (optional)

Rub the fat side of the rib roast with salt, pepper, and garlic powder. Place the roast on the mirepoix in a roasting pan, rib side down, add a little water for gravy, and bake in a preheated oven at 450° for 15 minutes. Turn the heat down to 325° and finish roasting to your taste (see note). Strain the fat drippings from the pan before you deglaze it, and if there is not enough gravy, add some beef base and a bit of sherry to stretch it. Slice the roast and serve with Yorkshire pudding and horseradish sauce (recipes follow).

Serves 4 to 8

Note: For rare, roast for approximately 11 minutes per pound, or to an interior temperature of 125°; for medium, approximately 12 minutes per pound, or 140°; for well done, approximately 13 minutes per pound, or 150°.

YORKSHIRE PUDDING

1 1/2 cups flour
1/2 teaspoon pepper
1 teaspoon nutmeg
1 teaspoon salt
4 eggs
1 1/2 cups milk
2 cups fat drippings from roasting pan

Combine all of the dry ingredients and mix well. Beat the eggs and milk and mix in the dry ingredients. (This can be done in a food processor.) Blend until smooth. Cover and refrigerate for 2 hours.

Preheat the oven to 450°. Use a muffin tin and fill each compartment one third full of fat drippings. Set the tin in the oven. Remove the batter from the refrigerator and beat again to ensure smoothness. When the fat smokes, add the batter to the muffin tin, filling it no more than two thirds full. Bake for 15 minutes at 450°; then reduce the heat to 300° and bake for another 15 minutes. Do not open the oven door until the pudding is done, or it will fall.

Serves 8

HORSERADISH SAUCE

- 1 cup heavy cream or crème fraîche
- 1 tablespoon lemon juice
- 1 tablespoon chopped fresh parsley
- 4 tablespoons grated fresh horseradish, or 8 tablespoons prepared horseradish
- Salt
- Pepper

Beat the cream to the soft-peaks stage. Add the remaining ingredients. Adjust the seasoning and serve.

Serves 4 to 8

Variation: Add 1 or 2 dashes of Worcestershire sauce.

BAKED RIBS OF BEEF DIJONNAISE

- 2 tablespoons minced garlic
- 2 tablespoons chopped fresh parsley
- 1 tablespoon pepper
- 3 tablespoons melted butter
- Dijon mustard
- 7 ribs from cooked rib roast
- 3 cups bread crumbs

Combine the garlic, parsley, pepper, and butter. Spread mustard on the ribs and coat with bread crumbs. Bake in a preheated 375° oven until golden brown.

Serves 7 as an appetizer

RED FLANNEL HASH

- 2 eggs beaten with 1/4 cup milk
- Salt
- Pepper
- 2 tablespoons chopped fresh parsley
- 2 pounds beef trimmings, finely chopped

2 potatoes, peeled, blanched, and cut into 1/2-inch dice
1 onion, cut into 1/2-inch dice and briefly sautéed
2 beets, peeled, blanched, and cut into 1/2-inch dice

Combine the egg mixture with salt, pepper, and parsley. Add the remaining ingredients and combine well. Form into patties and fry in a heavy skillet until browned on both sides and thoroughly heated. Serve plain or with poached or fried eggs.
Serves 8

HOT STEAK SALAD

Marinade

Salt
Pepper
2 large pinches of minced fresh sweet basil
2 dashes of Worcestershire sauce
2 pinches of oregano
2 tablespoons red or white vinegar
2 tablespoons olive oil
4 tablespoons red wine

12 ounces beef tips, thinly sliced, 2 to 3 inches long and 1/2 inch thick
Lettuce
Broccoli and cauliflower florets

Dipping Sauce

3 to 4 tablespoons mayonnaise
4 drops lemon juice
2 teaspoons minced onion
2 teaspoons minced fresh parsley
2 to 3 teaspoons dry white wine
Several dashes of dried dill

Combine the marinade ingredients. Marinate the beef tips and cook them in the marinade. Remove and serve on a bed of lettuce with raw cauliflower and broccoli florets on the side.

Whip together the ingredients for the dipping sauce. Pour into a bowl and set in the center of the dish you are serving the steak on. You can also use the marinade as a dipping sauce.

Serves 2

This is an unusual salad—a steak salad served hot, with pieces of fresh vegetables and a special sauce for the vegetables, along with the sauce the dish itself makes.

GRILLADES

- 1 1/2 pounds round steak, cut 1/2 inch thick
- Salt
- Pepper
- 1 tablespoon lard
- 1 onion, sliced
- 1 garlic clove, minced
- 1 tomato, chopped
- Parsley sprigs

Cut the meat into 4 squares or serving pieces. Season it with salt and pepper, rubbing them in thoroughly. Heat the lard in a heavy skillet and cook the onion and garlic until golden. Add the tomato and steak. Cover and cook slowly, turning occasionally, until brown and tender. Serve garnished with parsley.

Serves 4

THE HIDDEN-CHEESE BURGER

- 1 pound ground chuck
- Salt
- Pepper
- 2 tablespoons finely chopped fresh parsley
- 2 tablespoons steak sauce
- 1/4 pound grated cheese (your choice)

Mix the chuck, salt, pepper, parsley, and steak sauce. Form thick patties, then make a hole in each with your thumb. Fill the hole with cheese and cover with additional meat mixture. Reshape the patty, and fry to the desired doneness. Covering the pan will create steam and help keep your burger moist, and also melt the cheese.

Serves 4

ITALIAN MEATBALLS

- Salt
- Pepper
- 1/2 cup cream
- 1 tablespoon finely minced fresh parsley
- 1 tablespoon finely minced fresh basil
- 2 tablespoons grated Parmesan cheese
- 1 onion, finely minced
- 1 egg, beaten
- 2 garlic cloves, finely minced
- Bread crumbs, as needed
- 1 pound ground chuck
- Olive oil

Combine the salt, pepper, cream, parsley, basil, cheese, onion, egg, garlic, and bread crumbs. Blend thoroughly. Add the chuck and mix together. Form into 16 meatballs. Fry slowly in olive oil until done.

Serves 4

MEAT LOAF WITH DILL AND HARD-BOILED EGGS

- 1 egg, beaten
- Salt
- Pepper
- 2 tablespoons Worcestershire sauce
- 1 cup half-and-half
- 1/4 cup bread crumbs
- 2 tablespoons finely chopped fresh dill
- 2 pounds ground chuck
- 3 eggs, hard-boiled and peeled
- 8 strips bacon

Combine the beaten egg, salt, pepper, Worcestershire sauce, half-and-half, bread crumbs, dill, and chuck. Mix thoroughly. Trim the hard-boiled eggs at the ends so that they butt together to form one tubular egg. Shape the meat loaf so that it surrounds the eggs completely. Place the bacon strips over the loaf and tuck the ends under. Poke a few random holes through the bacon to allow steam to escape and bacon fat to drip into the loaf. Bake at 350° for 30 minutes, then at 500° long enough to crisp the bacon.

Serves 6 to 8

REAL SHEPHERD'S PIE

- 1 pound lean hamburger
- 1 large onion, finely chopped
- 1/2 teaspoon poultry seasoning
- Salt
- Pepper
- 4 large potatoes, peeled
- Cream or milk
- Butter
- 1 small can corn niblets
- 1 small can baby peas
- Paprika

Sauté the hamburger with the onion. Add the poultry seasoning and a bit of salt and pepper to taste. Cook the potatoes. Mash them with some cream or milk and just a bit of butter, if you like. Place the cooked hamburger in the bottom of a 5 × 10-inch casserole, about 2 inches high or even more. Cover half of the meat with corn and the other half with peas. Top with the mashed potatoes and dot with butter. Sprinkle the top with paprika. Bake at 350° until golden brown.

Serves 4

Veal

I feel that something should be said of this youngest and most tender of meats. Veal is the milk-fed meat of calves that are slaughtered no more than 12 weeks after birth. It has very little or no fat at all and a very high moisture content, so it will dry out quickly if left out too long or cooked too long. Even cooking it at too high a temperature is taboo. Veal has a delicate flavor and for this reason blends well with other foods as well as sauces. If cooked properly, veal will always be tender and cook quickly; it will display a fine appearance and texture when served. It is the gentlest of meats. So handle it gently, and the results will always be gratifying.

VEAL SCALLOPS, FRENCH STYLE

- 8 tablespoons (1 stick) butter
- 24 scalloped pieces of pounded veal, about the size of a silver dollar
- Flour
- 3 eggs, beaten lightly
- Juice of 2 lemons
- 1/2 cup Chablis

Melt the butter in a very large saucepan. Warm it gently. Pat the veal in flour. Dip in egg wash. Sauté lightly. Halfway through the first side's cooking, squeeze the lemon juice over the veal pieces. Turn them. Pour the wine over the second side, and finish sautéing the veal for but a few minutes. Remove the veal. Finish the sauce by reducing it just a bit. Pour it over the veal, serving 6 pieces per person.

Serves 4

SALTIMBOCCA

- 1 cup olive oil
- 4 very large slices veal
- 8 slices prosciutto
- 4 large slices mozzarella cheese
- Large amount of sage
- Butter
- 1/4 cup Madeira

Heat the oil in a large skillet. Sauté the veal on one side and remove. Pat each cooked side dry with paper towels and lay prosciutto and cheese on it. Fold the veal over and return it to the hot oil. Sprinkle sage on top of the veal. Sauté for a few minutes and remove. Drain most of the oil from the pan, add butter, heat it, and put the veal back in, cooked side up. Sprinkle sage on top and finish cooking (a few minutes). At the very end, add the wine. Remove the veal and deglaze the skillet. When the sauce is finished, pour it over the veal.

Serves 4

VEAL PAUPIETTES WITH OYSTERS

- 8 thin slices veal of equal size
- 1 cup soft bread crumbs
- 1/4 pound lean pork
- 1 tablespoon grated onion
- 1 tablespoon minced fresh parsley
- 1/2 teaspoon salt
- 1/8 teaspoon pepper
- 1/2 pint shucked oysters, with their liquor
- 4 slices bacon
- Melted butter
- 1/3 cup dry white wine (or more if needed)
- Minced fresh parsley for garnish

Have the butcher pound the meat to an even thickness and trim the slices to an even size and shape. Moisten the bread crumbs with cold water and gently squeeze out the excess. Put the pork through the finest blade of a meat grinder and combine with the bread crumbs. Blend the onion, parsley, salt, and pepper thoroughly. Spread a portion of this mixture evenly over each slice of veal. Poach the oysters in their liquor until plump; drain. Chop them and spread over the pork mixture.

Cut the bacon slices in half and lay half a slice crosswise over the oysters at one end of each veal slice. Roll up the slices, starting at the end with the bacon, so that the bacon will be at the middle of each paupiette. Tie the rolls several times around with thread. Brush with melted butter and lay side by side in a shallow baking dish. Brush the tops with more butter, and sprinkle lightly with additional salt and pepper. Bake at 325° for 1 hour, basting with the remaining butter every 10 to 15 minutes. Baste with the pan juices as they accumulate. Add a few tablespoons of hot water to the pan if there are signs of charring. When the veal is done, slip the baking pan under the broiler for 1 to 2 minutes to brown on top. Remove to a heated platter. Place the baking dish on top of the stove over moderate heat. Add the wine and swish it around, scraping up any browned bits. Add a pinch of salt and pepper if necessary, and when the liquid in the pan has been reduced to several spoonfuls, pour it over the paupiettes and sprinkle with minced parsley. Serve immediately.

Serves 4

CASHEWED VEAL BIRDS

- 4 slices cubed soft bread
- 1/2 teaspoon crushed coriander seeds
- 1/8 teaspoon curry powder
- 1/2 cup honey
- 1/2 teaspoon celery salt
- 1 cup finely chopped cashews
- 1 cup sauterne
- 8 slices veal, pounded thin
- 1 cup chicken or veal stock
- 1 cup heavy cream

Mix the bread, coriander seeds, curry powder, honey, celery salt, cashews, and most of the wine into a stuffing. Spread evenly on the slices of veal and roll them into a hot-dog shape. Place in a baking pan, moisten with a bit of stock, cover the pan, and bake at 375° for 15 to 20 minutes. Serve 2 stuffed birds on each dinner plate, with a sauce made with the cream, stock, and a bit of wine. Season it to taste with salt and white pepper, if you wish.

Serves 4

VEAL SCALOPPINE MILANESE

- Flour
- 24 pieces of veal (cut into 2-inch squares)
- Mixture of oil and butter
- 1 pound thinly sliced mushrooms
- 2 tablespoons chopped fresh parsley
- 1 cup peeled, seeded, diced fresh tomatoes
- 1/2 cup Marsala
- 1 garlic clove, pressed
- 2 tablespoons freshly chopped sweet basil
- 4 tablespoons grated Romano cheese

Flour the veal and sauté it in the mixture of oil and butter. Mix in the remaining ingredients, place in a large covered casserole dish, and bake in a preheated 375° oven for 15 to 20 minutes. Serve with noodles.

Serves 4

VEAL CARMEN

- 1 onion, chopped
- 2 shallots, finely chopped
- Mixture of oil and butter
- 1 cup sliced mushrooms
- 6 tomatoes, peeled, seeded, and chopped
- 1/4 cup Chablis
- 1 teaspoon tarragon
- 1/2 teaspoon sugar
- 1/4 teaspoon rosemary
- Flour
- 4 large veal cutlets
- Juice of 1/2 lemon
- 1 cup chicken or veal stock
- 1/4 teaspoon prepared mustard
- Several slices mozzarella cheese

Sauté the onion and shallots in the mixture of oil and butter. Add the mushrooms and cook until they begin to change color. Add the tomatoes and simmer for 5 minutes. Add the wine, tarragon, sugar, and rosemary and cook for 15 minutes.

Flour the veal and lightly brown it in the oil-butter mixture in another pan. Remove; add the lemon juice and stock to the pan and reduce it by half. Blend the mustard into the sautéed onion mixture, add the reduced stock, and put in a casserole dish with the veal. Top with the cheese, then bake in a preheated 400° oven for 15 minutes or more, until the cheese melts.

Serves 4

VEAL AND EGGPLANT PARMIGIANA

- 4 veal cutlets
- Flour
- 4 eggs, slightly beaten
- 1 can Italian bread crumbs
- Mixture of oil and butter
- 2 eggplants
- 1 quart spaghetti sauce
- 1 cup grated Romano cheese
- 8 slices Romano cheese

Pound the veal cutlets until thin. Flour them, dip them in egg wash, then in bread crumbs, and sauté in the mixture of oil and butter until just barely cooked. Slice the eggplants lengthwise, flour them, dip them in egg wash and bread crumbs, and sauté until just lightly browned on each side. In individual oven casserole dishes, place a bit of sauce on the bottom, put slices of the eggplant on it, veal on it, eggplant on the veal, then a bit more sauce, and top with a sprinkling of grated cheese and 2 cheese slices. Bake the casseroles in a preheated 400° oven until the cheese melts and becomes a nice rich golden brown. Place the casserole dishes on small platters and serve. Serve the remaining sauce on the side.

Serves 4

Note: If the casserole dishes are too small to hold the cutlets in one piece, cut them and the eggplants into strips.

VEAL PAPRIKASH

- 4 tablespoons butter
- 1/2 cup finely chopped onion
- 1 green pepper, very thinly sliced
- 1 tablespoon flour
- 1 tablespoon paprika
- 1 1/2 cups chicken stock
- 1/8 teaspoon sugar
- Salt
- Pepper
- 1 egg yolk
- 1/2 cup sour cream
- 2 cups cooked veal, cut into small cubes, then flattened
- 2 tablespoons minced fresh dill
- 1/4 teaspoon lemon juice

Melt the butter, heat slightly, and sauté the onion, then the green pepper, until done. Mix in the flour and paprika and cook slightly. Slowly add the chicken stock, making a sauce. Turn the heat down to a simmer; add the sugar and a bit of salt and pepper. Let this cook for about 10 minutes. Mix the egg yolk and sour cream and stir into the hot sauce, a bit at a time. Do not let it come to a boil. Add the veal and dill, heat it through, then add the lemon juice to the whole thing. Serve over egg noodles.

Serves 4

Pork

PORK TENDERLOIN VÉRONIQUE

- 2 whole pork tenderloins
- Mixture of oil and butter
- 2 leeks, white part only
- 2 celery stalks
- 1 parsnip, finely minced
- 1 small onion, minced
- 4 parsley sprigs, finely chopped
- 1 cup dry white wine
- 1 cup pork stock
- Roux (equal parts flour and butter, cooked)
- 1 very large bunch seedless white grapes

Slice the tenderloins into 24 large pieces. Heat the oil and butter mixture in a heated skillet and sauté the pork very lightly, just 1 to 2 minutes on each side. Remove from the pan. Add the leeks, celery, parsnip, onion, parsley, wine, and stock to the pan. Bring to a boil and simmer for at least 10 minutes. Thicken with the roux, checking for seasoning. (If there is any undue sharpness, add a bit of sweet white wine.) Turn off the heat and set the meat in the sauce for a few minutes. Remove the meat, reheat the sauce, and add the grapes, whole or halved. Place the sauce with the grapes on dinner plates. Lay 4 slices of meat, overlapping each other, on each portion of sauce and serve.

Serve 6

PORK CHOW YOK

- 1 pound pork tenderloin
- 1 tablespoon dark soy sauce
- 1 tablespoon hoisin sauce
- 2 tablespoons sweet sake
- 1 tablespoon dark brown sugar
- 2 eggs, beaten
- Flour
- Oil for deep-frying

Cut the meat into thin strips and flatten them. Soak them overnight in a mixture of soy sauce, hoisin sauce, sake, and sugar.

Dip the meat in the egg wash, then the flour, and fry in deep oil. Serve with Graham Kerr's steamed rice (page 136).

Serves 4

BAKED STUFFED PORK CHOPS

- 1 onion, minced
- 6 tablespoons raisins
- 2 eggs, beaten
- 2 tablespoons chopped fresh parsley
- 1/4 cup milk
- 6 tablespoons chopped pineapple
- 2 celery stalks, minced
- 6 slices bread
- 1/2 teaspoon sage
- 6 double-thick pork chops
- 2 tablespoons butter
- 2 cups pork stock
- Roux (equal parts flour and butter, cooked)

Mix the onion, raisins, eggs, parsley, milk, pineapple, celery, bread, and sage into a stuffing. If it is too moist, add more bread; if too dry, add a bit of stock. Cut a large pocket into the center of each chop and fill with the stuffing. Melt the butter in a skillet and brown the chops lightly on both sides, then place them in a roasting pan. Put some of the stock in the pan and bake the chops at 350° for an hour or more, basting often. Remove the chops when done. Deglaze the pan on top of the stove and thicken it with the roux. Serve the chops with a generous amount of sauce.

Serves 6

CREOLE PORK CHOPS

- 12 small (6-ounce) pork chops
- 1 cup flour
- Salt
- Pepper
- Just enough salad oil to cover the bottom of a large skillet
- Creole sauce (page 252)

Dredge the chops in a mixture of flour, salt, pepper. Heat a skillet, heat a film of oil in it, and brown the chops on both sides. Put the chops in a large casserole dish, cover with creole sauce, and bake at 325° until the pork is tender. Serve with plain rice.

Serves 6

A HONEY OF A PORK CHOP

- Oil
- 12 small pork chops
- 1/2 cup applesauce
- 1 tablespoon hoisin sauce
- 2 tablespoons dark brown sugar
- 4 ounces light honey
- 2 jiggers apple liqueur

Heat a skillet, heat a little oil in it, and brown the chops on both sides. Remove the chops, add the remaining ingredients, and bring to a simmer. Cook for a few minutes, then remove from the heat. Put the chops in a large casserole dish, cover with the sauce, and bake, covered, at 375° for 30 minutes. Remove the cover and cook at 325° until the chops are tender. Serve the chops with the sauce over them.

Serves 6

MEDALLIONS OF PORK CALVADOS

- 8 medallions of pork
- 1 teaspoon finely minced shallots
- 1 tablespoon Dijon mustard
- 1/2 cup Calvados (apple brandy)
- 1 cup heavy cream
- 1 apple, cored and sliced into rings
- 1 tablespoon finely chopped fresh parsley

Sauté the medallions, remove them, and keep in a warm place. Remove excess fat from the pan and add the shallots, mustard, and Calvados. Reduce until almost dry. Add the cream and bring to a boil. Add the apple rings and parsley. Reduce until the sauce thickens. Pour over the medallions and serve.

Serves 2

ROAST PORK

- 1 butt end of pork loin (5 to 6 pounds), ready for roasting
- 6 garlic cloves
- Salt
- Pepper
- 2 cups mirepoix (coarsely chopped celery, carrots, and onions)
- 2 cups water
- Roux (equal parts flour and butter, cooked)

Looking directly down on the roast, cut 6 small pockets and insert the garlic. Sprinkle the roast with salt and pepper. Place the mirepoix and water in a pan and set the roast on it. Cook at 350° for approximately 1½ hours. Strain the juices, deglaze the pan, and mix with the roux for gravy.

Serves 4

SWEET AND SOUR PORK

- 1 cup vinegar
- 1 pint sugar
- 3½ cups water
- 6 to 8 tablespoons cornstarch
- 1 cup sweet relish
- 1 to 2 tablespoons soy sauce
- 4 tablespoons rice wine
- 1 teaspoon chopped or grated ginger root
- 1½ to 2 pounds boneless pork, cut into strips ½ inch thick and 3 to 4 inches long

Mix the vinegar, sugar, and 2¾ cups water, put in a pot, and boil for 4 or 5 minutes. Dissolve the cornstarch in the remaining water, add to the pot, and whip until smooth and stiff. Add the relish, soy sauce, and rice wine, stirring constantly with a wooden spoon. Add the ginger, simmer for a short time, then remove from the heat. Add the pork and let it marinate for 10 to 15 minutes. In a wok or large skillet, cook the pork in the marinade. Serve over rice.

Serves 4

PORK TERIYAKI

- 1 pound cubed pork
- 2 tablespoons brown sugar
- 1/2 onion, finely minced
- 1/2 cup shoyu sauce
- 2 tablespoons sake
- 1/2 garlic clove, finely minced

Cut the pork into large cubes and marinate overnight in a sauce made from the other ingredients. Broil the pork slowly on a charcoal grill, basting and turning as often as seems necessary. Serve with rice.

Serves 4

PORK KNUCKLES IN SAUCE

- 4 pork knuckles
- 1 cup pork stock
- 1 garlic clove, crushed or minced
- 1/2 tablespoon brown sugar
- 2 tablespoons sake
- Pepper
- 2 to 3 tablespoons cornstarch dissolved in 1/4 cup cold water

Put the knuckles in a pot of water, bring to a boil, and cook, covered at a low boil until well done. Remove them from the pot and bone them. The meat will come right off if they are well cooked.

In another pot, mix the stock, garlic, sugar, sake, and pepper. Bring to a rapid boil and let it reduce for at least 5 minutes.

Thicken with the cornstarch paste using enough to make the stock semithick. Add the pork, heat through, and serve.
Serves 4

BROILED HAWAIIAN HAM STEAK

	Oil		Sprinkling of cinnamon
1	ham steak	2	pineapple rings
1	tablespoon brown sugar	1	maraschino cherry

Oil the bottom of a broiling pan. Broil the ham steak on high, browning each side. Remove from the broiler and keep hot. Combine the sugar and cinnamon. Place the pineapple rings in a shallow baking pan and put the cherry in the center. Sprinkle the sugar mixture on top and broil, turning once, until browned on both sides. Place the rings on the ham and spoon the juice from the baking pan on top.
Serves 1

CREAMED HAM ON A CROISSANT

16 to 24	ounces cooked ham		Roux (equal parts flour and butter, cooked)
2	tablespoons butter or 4 tablespoons ham stock	1	package frozen peas
2	cups half-and-half	4	large or 8 small croissants

Cut the ham into bite-size pieces. Sauté in a bit of butter or the ham stock until hot. Add the half-and-half, thicken with the roux, and add the peas. Heat through. To serve, cut the croissants in half and ladle on some of the creamed ham.
Serves 4

Lamb

*L*amb is not only very economical but delicious. Prepared properly, it can be a blessing when you are at your wits' end trying to cook something different, wholesome, and pleasing.

First, learn the type of cuts and how to cook them.

The leg can be purchased as a whole. You can have the butcher cut several lamb steaks from it and have an extra dinner in the future.

The chops and T-bones are the smaller rib section. If you are inclined really to put on the dog, have the butcher make a nice crown roast for you.

The shanks are the foreleg. You can bake them in a special marinade and really make a guest's mouth water.

The shoulder is the least expensive cut, but you can stuff it and have a real beauty of a roast.

THE DINGO ROAST LEG OF LAMB

2 garlic cloves, minced
2 tablespoons lemon juice
Salt
Pepper
2 bay leaves, finely crumbled
Large pinch of thyme
Several leaves of fresh dill
1 tablespoon wine vinegar
1 leg of lamb, about 6 to 8 pounds
4 whole garlic cloves
2 cups mirepoix (coarsely chopped celery, carrots, and onions)
Roux (equal parts flour and butter, cooked)

Mix the minced garlic, lemon juice, salt, pepper, bay, thyme, dill, and vinegar. Make 4 holes in the leg and insert the whole garlic cloves. Rub the entire leg with the mixture of the seasonings and place the leg in a roasting pan, setting it on the mirepoix. Add a small amount of water. Roast at 425° for 15 minutes, then turn the oven down to 325° and roast the leg to doneness, figuring about 1 1/2 hours for rare, 2 1/2 hours for medium, and so on. (To check for doneness, insert a metal fork into the meaty part of the leg, leave it in for a slow count of five, take it out, and touch your lip with it. If it is cold, the meat is raw; just slightly warm, very rare. The more heat you feel, the more the leg is cooked. It's really that easy.) Add water as needed, and put in enough to make gravy later.

Once the roast is done, remove it and deglaze the pan over a stove burner. Add more water, if needed, and thicken with the roux. Strain this through a sieve or strainer and you have your gravy. Serve it with the roast and you have a beautiful dinner.

Serves 10 to 12

THE HAWAIIAN DECAMBRA LEG ROAST

- 1 leg of lamb, boned
- 1/4 teaspoon marjoram
- 1/4 teaspoon thyme
- 1 tablespoon mild prepared mustard
- 1/2 teaspoon each grated orange and lemon zest
- 1/2 cup orange juice
- 1/2 cup pineapple juice
- 1 small onion, chopped
- 1 jigger Tokay wine
- 4 sprigs parsley
- 2 to 4 tablespoons arrowroot powder (optional)

Rub the leg of lamb with the seasonings and herbs. Place in a pan. Add the remaining ingredients, except the arrowroot, to the pan. Roast at 425° for 15 to 20 minutes. Turn the heat down to 325° and finish to the desired doneness. Be certain to baste the lamb frequently. Remove the lamb from the pan and strain the stock. If you wish to thicken the stock, mix arrowroot with a bit of water, heat the stock, and thicken as you like.

Serves 6

Stafford L. DeCambra is head chef instructor at the University of Hawaii.

LAMB CHOPS DU BARRY

- 12 small lamb chops
- Butter
- 4 tablespoons water
- 4 tablespoons white wine
- 1 package or bunch fresh mint, very finely chopped
- 4 tablespoons sugar
- 4 tablespoons mint jelly
- Applesauce

You can broil or charbroil lamb chops, but for this dish I suggest pan-frying in butter. When done, remove. Deglaze the pan with the water and wine. Add the mint. Sauté for a few minutes, then add the sugar and mint jelly over a low flame. When the sauce is done, strain it through a sieve. Serve the sauce all over the chops, with applesauce on the side.

Serves 6

LAMB CHOPS WITH FETA CHEESE, OLIVES, AND TOMATO SAUCE

- Greek olive oil
- 6 thick loin lamb chops
- 2 garlic cloves, minced
- 1 small onion, minced
- Several pinches of oregano
- 1 cup good Greek wine (retsina)
- Salt
- Pepper
- 18 chopped black Greek olives
- 1 cup chopped peeled tomatoes
- 1/2 pound feta cheese

*H*eat the oil and sauté the chops in a pan until just done. Add the garlic and onion and sauté for a few minutes. Do not brown them. Add the oregano, wine, salt, and pepper. Turn the heat down to low and cook the chops until just tender, which should take no more than half an hour. Remove the chops from the pan. Add the olives and tomatoes and cook for a few minutes. Mix in the feta cheese and serve over the chops.

Serves 6

CROWN ROAST OF LAMB WITH SIX VEGETABLES

- 1 crown roast
- Olive oil
- Salt
- Pepper
- 16 cherry tomatoes
- 1 bunch broccoli
- 16 medium-sized mushrooms
- 16 round potatoes, about 1 1/2 inches in diameter
- 1 head cauliflower
- 4 carrots, cut into 1-inch rounds
- Mint sauce (page 255)

Rub the roast with oil and salt and pepper. Wrap pieces of aluminum foil around the tips of the bones so they will not burn. Cook the roast in a large pan in a 360° oven (15 minutes per pound for a rare roast). On the side, cook all the vegetables. The tomatoes can be blanched for a few minutes. (You can cook them longer if you prefer, but keep in mind that vegetables should not be overcooked.)

Remove the roast from the oven. Take off the foil and replace it with paper panties. Fill the center of the roast with the vegetables, intermixed. Serve with mint sauce.

Serves 8

BRAISED BREAST OF LAMB

- 1 5- to 6-pound breast of lamb
- Oil
- Salt
- Pepper
- 2 bay leaves, crumbled
- 1 cup mirepoix (chopped celery, carrots, and onions)
- 1/2 teaspoon marjoram
- 1/4 cup tomato purée
- Lamb stock
- Roux (equal parts flour and butter, cooked)

Rub the breast with oil, salt, pepper, and bay leaves. Place it in a pan. In a 425° oven, roast until slightly browned. Add the mirepoix, marjoram, tomato purée, and stock. Cover the pan and turn the oven down to 325°. Braise the roast until it is very tender. Remove the breast and deglaze the pan on top of the stove. Thicken it with the roux and strain the gravy.

Serves 6

ROAST STUFFED LAMB

Bread Stuffing

3 celery stalks
1 large onion
1 garlic clove, minced or pressed
4 tablespoons butter
2 cups diced bread or unflavored croutons
4 tablespoons Tokay
Crushed peppercorns to taste
1 tablespoon caraway seeds
4 pounds boned lamb shoulder, all fat trimmed off
Oil
1 teaspoon dried rosemary
Salt
Pepper
2 cups mirepoix (chopped celery, carrots, and onions)
1 quart lamb or beef stock
Roux (equal parts flour and butter, cooked)

Sauté the celery, onion, and garlic in the butter. Add to the bread cubes and mix in the Tokay, peppercorns, and caraway seeds.

Stuff the shoulder and tie it with twine. Rub it with the oil, rosemary, salt, and pepper. Roast at 325° for at least 2 hours. Add the mirepoix and the stock. Rotate the lamb and cook for another half hour. Remove the lamb. Thicken the stock with the roux and strain it. To serve, slice the lamb and set it down on the gravy, or serve the gravy on the side.

Serves 6 to 8

O'SHAUGHNESSY'S IRISH STEW

3 pounds cubed lamb from the shoulder
3 large carrots, cut into bite-size pieces
6 small potatoes, cut in half
1 very small turnip
6 pearl onions

- 2 leeks, white part only, cut up
- 1/4 teaspoon marjoram
- Salt
- Pepper to taste
- Butter
- 1 small package frozen mixed vegetables
- Roux (equal parts flour and butter, cooked)

Put the meat, carrots, and potatoes in a large pot, cover with water, and bring to a boil. Turn the heat down to a simmer and cook until the meat is tender. Skim off the excess grease with a skimmer and paper towels. Cook the turnip separately. Add it to the pot. Sauté the onions, leeks, marjoram, salt, and pepper in butter. Add to the pot and simmer for about 15 minutes, to incorporate all the flavors. Add the frozen mixed vegetables and let everything simmer for 5 minutes. Strain the contents into another pot, thicken the stock with the roux, and put everything back together.

Serves 6

LAMB FRICASSEE

- 3 pounds lamb, cut into 1-inch cubes
- Roux (equal parts flour and butter, cooked)
- 1/4 cup chopped fresh mint
- Salt
- Pepper

Cook the lamb in 2 quarts water until tender. Skim the top, then strain the stock and thicken it with the roux. Replace the meat. Add the mint and reheat. Season and serve over noodles.

Serves 6

INDIA'S CURRIED LAMB

- 1 shoulder of lamb (about 4 pounds)
- 2 quarts lamb stock
- 1 small onion, chopped
- 1/2 cup mirepoix (celery, carrots, and onions cut into 1/2-inch dice)
- Butter

- 1/2 cup flour
- 2 tablespoons hot curry powder
- 1 teaspoon cumin
- 1/4 teaspoon powdered cloves
- 1 tablespoon chopped fresh fennel or teaspoon fennel seeds
- 3 tablespoons grated coconut
- 1 teaspoon grated orange zest
- 1/2 teaspoon grated lemon zest
- 3 tablespoons brown sugar
- 1 large apple, cored and cut into small dice
- 1 banana, puréed

Cube the lamb and cook it in the stock. Skim the stock; remove the lamb. In a large pot, sauté the onion and mirepoix in butter. Mix the flour, curry powder, cumin, cloves, fennel, and coconut. Add to the pot and cook slightly. Add the stock slowly and cook for a few minutes. Purée in a food processor or a blender and return to the pot. Add the zests, meat, and sugar. Ten or 15 minutes later, add the apple and cook for a few minutes, then add the bananas. Bake in a covered casserole dish at 360° until the lamb is very tender. Serve over rice.

Serves 6

MARY'S LAMB SHANKS IN SAUCE

- 4 lamb shanks
- Juice of 1/2 lemon
- 2 garlic cloves, minced
- 1 cup flour
- 1 teaspoon salt
- 1 teaspoon pepper
- 1/2 cup mild salad oil
- 2 cups beef stock
- 1/2 cup dry vermouth
- 1/2 cup water
- 1 large onion, finely minced
- 2 large carrots, cut into bite-size pieces
- 2 celery stalks, cut into bite-size pieces

Rub the shanks with lemon juice and garlic. Set aside for at least a half hour.

Mix the flour, salt, and pepper and rub the shanks with the mixture. Save the rest of the flour for thickening the sauce.

Brown the shanks in oil. Take them out of the pan; add the remaining flour and cook into a roux for the sauce. Add the beef stock, vermouth, and water. Stir until smooth. (If it does not become smooth, strain it.) Add the onion and cook. Place the shanks and sauce in a baking dish and cook in a 325° oven for 2 hours.

Turn the shanks over and add the carrots and celery to the dish. Put it back in the oven and bake for about another hour, until you can feel the tenderness of the shanks. Serve with buttered noodles on the side.

Serves 4

GREEK LAMB CURRY

- 2 onions, sliced
- 3 garlic cloves, chopped
- 4 tablespoons melted butter
- Juice of 1 lemon
- Salt
- Pepper
- 1/2 teaspoon curry powder, or more to taste
- 1/4 cup flour
- 3 cups cubed cooked lamb
- 4 tablespoons Madeira
- 1 1/2 cups chicken stock

Sauté the onions and garlic in butter in the bottom of a casserole dish. Use the lemon juice to wet the meat. Mix the salt, pepper, and curry powder with the flour, and roll the lamb in it. Take the onion and garlic out of the casserole, add a bit more butter for frying, and lightly brown the lamb. Add the onions and garlic and the remaining ingredients, then cover the dish and bake at 360° for about an hour. The whole thing should be thickened enough from flouring the meat. However, if it is not thick enough, you can thicken it a bit more with a roux (equal parts flour and butter, cooked).

Serves 6

A good way to use leftover lamb.

POULTRY

Chicken and a Turkey

Chickens are likely to be contaminated with salmonella, so wash them well, inside and out, in salted water with a little vinegar.

ROAST CHICKEN

- 1 6- to 8-pound roaster
- Salt
- Pepper to taste
- 1 small jar mayonnaise

Wash the chicken and dry it well. Rub the chicken inside and out with salt, pepper, and mayonnaise. Bake at 375° until crusty brown (which will be accomplished by the mayonnaise on the chicken skin), 10 to 12 minutes per pound. That's it!

Serves 4 to 6

CHICKEN BREASTS DIPPED IN HONEY WITH CRUSHED ALMONDS (POULETTE ALMONDE DE VIN)

- 4 boneless, skinless chicken breasts, flattened
- 1 pint light honey (not dark)
- 8 ounces almonds, chopped and crushed
- 4 tablespoons butter
- 2 tablespoons lemon juice
- 1/4 cup sauterne
- 1 pint heavy cream

Dip the breasts in honey, then coat with almonds. Sauté in butter until done, approximately 4 minutes per side. Remove the breasts and deglaze the pan with lemon juice and sauterne. Add the cream, reduce the heat, and cook until the sauce is as thick as a cream sauce. Serve over the chicken.

Serves 4

CHICKEN PALOISE

- 1 2 1/2-pound chicken, cut into 8 pieces
- Salt
- Pepper
- 4 tablespoons olive oil
- 3 tomatoes, peeled and chopped
- 3 green peppers, seeded and sliced lengthwise
- 2 garlic cloves, crushed
- 1 cup sliced mushrooms
- 1/4 pound cooked ham, diced
- 1/2 cup dry white wine
- 3 tablespoons armagnac or cognac
- Chopped fresh parsley

Season the chicken pieces with salt and pepper. Heat the olive oil in a heavy casserole or saucepan and sauté the chicken until golden brown, about 10 minutes. Add the tomatoes, green peppers, garlic, mushrooms, ham, and wine. Cover and cook gently for half an hour, or until the chicken is tender. Remove the chicken to a hot platter, blend the sauce with a whisk, and reduce it until fairly thick. Return the chicken to the pan, pour armagnac over it, and ignite. Let the flames die out and sprinkle with parsley.

Serves 8

CHINESE-HAWAIIAN CHICKEN ANISE

- 8 tablespoons melted chicken fat (see note)
- 2 3- to 4-pound chickens, disjointed
- 8 small scallions, cut into 1-inch lengths
- 2 tablespoons dark brown sugar
- 4 tablespoons soy sauce
- 2/3 cup anisette or Pernod
- 2 cups chicken stock

Heat the fat in a large skillet. Brown the chicken pieces well on all sides and remove from the skillet. Add the scallions to the skillet and sprinkle with sugar and soy sauce. Combine the liqueur and stock, return the chicken to the skillet, and pour the liqueur mixture over it. Cook, uncovered, over low heat for 30 minutes. Turn the heat to high and cook, several pieces of chicken at a time, until the skin is browned and crisp. The liquid will boil off almost entirely. Serve with plain or fried rice, if you wish.

Serves 12

Note: Pick off any pieces of fat from the chickens and melt them in a small frying pan. If there is not enough to make 8 tablespoons, add safflower oil to make up the difference.

CHICKEN WITH MINT AND ORANGE SAUCE

- 5 mint sprigs plus more for garnish
- 1 3- to 3 1/2-pound chicken
- 4 tablespoons softened butter
- Salt
- Pepper
- 2 tablespoons Grand Marnier
- 1/4 cup orange juice
- 1/2 cup chicken stock
- 1/2 stick (4 tablespoons) cold butter, cubed
- 2 tablespoons chopped fresh mint
- 1 teaspoon grated orange zest
- Orange slices

Put 5 mint sprigs in the cavity of the chicken and truss to close it up. Rub the skin with softened butter and season with salt and pepper. Place the chicken, breast side up, on a rack in a preheated 450° oven and immediately reduce the heat to 350°. Roast for 1 to 1 1/4 hours, basting every 15 minutes.

Place the chicken on a warm platter and remove the mint sprigs from the cavity. Pour off excess fat from the roasting pan. On top of stove deglaze the pan with the remaining juices and Grand Marnier. Add the orange juice and chicken stock and bring to a boil, stirring to pick up any roasted bits left in the pan. Transfer the liquid to a small heavy saucepan and reduce by half over high heat. You should have about 1/2 cup. Remove from the heat and whisk in the cold butter, a piece at a time. Add the chopped mint and grated zest. Put the chicken on a platter and garnish with orange slices and mint sprigs. Serve the sauce separately.

Serves 4

CHICKEN OR TURKEY TETRAZZINI

1 pound fettuccine noodles or spaghetti
About 2 tablespoons olive oil
1 small onion, minced
2 garlic cloves, minced
1 quart heavy cream
8 to 12 ounces grated Parmesan cheese
8 medium-size mushrooms, thinly sliced
Roux (equal parts flour and butter, cooked) (optional)
18 to 24 ounces cooked chicken or turkey meat

Cook the noodles *al dente.* In a large saucepan, heat the olive oil and sauté the onion, then the garlic, until just done. Add the cream, heat, and whip in three fourths of the cheese. In a skillet, sauté the mushrooms in a little oil until completely cooked. If you like, thicken the cheese sauce slightly with the roux. Add the mushrooms. Slice the chicken or turkey meat into strips about 1/4 inch thick and 2 to 3 inches long. Add to the sauce and mix well. Mix the sauce with the noodles, place in individual casserole dishes, and top with the remaining cheese. Bake in a 350° oven only until the top shows a slight browning, then remove and serve.

Serves 6 to 8

Leftovers? There is no such thing. There may be slices or pieces of chicken or turkey left from the original meal, but don't let anyone tell you that these are leftovers and shouldn't be served to honored guests. Here is a dish I would serve my most revered of friends with pride. You should not feel any embarrassment about using things that were part of another meal. If you had to make the dish from scratch, you would have to cook the meat first anyway. See what I mean?

ROAST TURKEY WITH STUFFING

- 1 10-pound turkey
- Salt
- Pepper
- Poultry seasoning
- 1 bunch parsley
- 6 celery stalks, coarsely chopped
- 3 onions, coarsely chopped
- 4 carrots, coarsely chopped
- 2 cups water

Wash the turkey and pat dry. Season the cavity with salt, pepper, and poultry seasoning. Put the parsley and half of the celery, onions, and carrots in the cavity. Put the other half in a roasting pan, along with the water. Place the turkey in the pan, cover it with a foil tent, and set it in a 325°oven. Roast for approximately 3 hours. Remove the foil and baste the turkey with the pan juices every 10 minutes until it is golden brown. To check for doneness, insert a fork into the thigh. If the liquid runs clear, the turkey is done. Serve with one of the following stuffings.

Serves 6 to 8

Chestnut Stuffing

- 1 loaf white bread, crusts trimmed off, cut into cubes
- 1/2 cup milk
- 2 tablespoons rubbed sage
- 1 large onion, cut into 1/2-inch dice
- 6 celery stalks, cut into 1/2-inch dice
- 1 can chestnuts, chopped
- 1/2 cup white wine
- Salt
- Pepper
- Melted butter

Soak the bread cubes in milk. Combine with the sage, onion, celery, chestnuts, wine, salt, and pepper. Turn it into a buttered baking dish, drizzle with melted butter, and bake in a 350° oven for approximately 1 hour, until the top is browned.

Serves 6 to 8

Ground Beef and Mashed Potato Stuffing

- 1 pound ground beef, cooked and crumbled
- Salt
- Pepper
- 1 onion, cut into 1/2-inch dice
- 1 tablespoon poultry seasoning
- 3 cups mashed potatoes
- Melted butter

Combine the beef, salt, pepper, onion, poultry seasoning, and mashed potatoes. Turn into a buttered baking dish, drizzle with melted butter, and bake in a 350° oven for approximately 1/2 hour, until browned.

Serves 6 to 8

Sausage Stuffing

- 1 box seasoned croutons
- 1/2 pound ground sausage, cooked and crumbled
- 1 tablespoon poultry seasoning
- 1 tablespoon rubbed sage
- 1/2 cup white wine
- 1 cup diced red and green peppers
- 1 small onion, diced
- 2 celery stalks, diced

Prepare as in the previous recipe.

Serves 6 to 8

Duck and Game Birds

*M*ost of us are quite familiar with turkey, chicken, and even Cornish game hen, but not too many of us have done much with duck, goose, guinea hen, pheasant, grouse, quail, or partridge. The following recipes can be used with any of them.

ROAST WILD DUCK, AMERICAN INDIAN STYLE

1 4- to 5-pound wild duck
1 cup plain, uncooked maple sap, or 1/4 cup maple syrup mixed with hot water
1 teaspoon sea salt
1 tablespoon black peppercorns
Large handful of wild scallions or fresh chives
Husks of 12 ears of corn

Rub the duck with the sap, then with the salt. Place the peppercorns and scallions in the cavity of the bird. Wrap the duck with the corn husks and bake in a preheated oven at 325° for 21/2 to 3 hours.

Remove the bird from the oven; strain the juices from the pan and set aside. Place the bird on a racked pan, put it back in the oven, and bake it to a crispy stage. Serve the bird, thinly sliced, with some of the strained juices on it.

Serves 4

ROAST PEKING DUCK

1 4- to 5-pound duck
4 tablespoons molasses
2 tablespoons rice wine
3 bunches scallions, white part only
4 tablespoons hoisin sauce

Wash the duck well, removing all the fat you can. Boil a large pot of water and dip the duck in the boiling water for about 5 minutes. Tie the duck up and hang it in a nice cool, airy spot for half a day. Mix the molasses, rice wine, and a bit of water, rub the duck with the mixture, then hang the duck overnight.

Preheat the oven to 350°. Place the duck on a rack in a roasting pan and roast for 11/2 hours. Raise the temperature to 425° and roast the duck for another 15 to 20 minutes. Take the bird out of the oven, skin it as best you can without ruining any of the meat, reserve the skin, and slice the meat into strips 2 to 3 inches long. Place the meat in the center of a serving platter, brush it with hoisin sauce, and lay the scallions over it. Cut the skin into strips and place around the meat.

Serves 4

PRESSED DUCK

- 1 4- to 5-pound duck
- 1 teaspoon saltpeter
- 6 tablespoons salt
- 2 tablespoons anise pepper

Wash the duck and remove all the fat you can, then dry it well. Mix the saltpeter, salt, and anise pepper and rub the duck with it, inside and out. Place the duck on a rack in a pan and refrigerate, covered, for 3 days, then hang it out in the sun for a day.

Cut the duck into quarters and wash away the salt mixture with cold water. Put the duck in a large steamer, place a weight on it, and steam it for at least an hour, turning it once or twice. You can then set it aside until you are ready to use it. It will keep for a week or even more, depending on good refrigeration.

When ready to use, either fry it in sesame oil, safflower oil, or the like, or just lightly sauté it.

Serves 4

DRUNKEN DUCK

- 1 4- to 5-pound duck
- 1 tablespoon minced garlic
- 3 tablespoons soy sauce
- 1/8 cup sugar
- 3 tablespoons chopped scallions
- 1/4 cup sesame oil
- 2 cups beer
- 3 tablespoons cornstarch, mixed with water

Remove the fat from the duck and wash it well, then dry it and cut it into quarters. Mix the garlic, soy sauce, sugar, and scallions and rub the mixture all over the duck. In a large pot, heat the oil, then sauté the duck quarters in it. Take the duck out of the pot; add beer to the pot and bring to a boil. Add the duck, reduce the heat, cover, and simmer for 1 to 1 1/2 hours. When you are sure the duck is done, take it out of the pot, strain the juices, and thicken with the cornstarch paste. Slice the duck into bite-size pieces and serve with the sauce.

Serves 4

SPICY GINGER DUCK

- 1 5- to 6-pound duck
- 4 tablespoons sesame oil
- 12 slices ginger root
- Zest of 1 orange, cut into pieces
- Cornstarch dissolved in cold water
- 8 tablespoons sake

Wash the duck, pull off all the fat, then dry the duck and cut it into pieces. Heat the oil in a large skillet, add the ginger and orange zest, and sauté the duck until a dark, rich golden brown. Remove the duck; strain the juices and thicken with the cornstarch paste. Strain through cheesecloth, add the sake and cook it down just a bit, then serve it with the duck.

Serves 4

SPICY STUFF-A-DUCK

- 1 5- to 6-pound duck
- 2 tablespoons ground coriander
- 1 teaspoon ground cumin
- 1/4 teaspoon saffron
- 1/2 teaspoon ground anise
- 2 teaspoons ground ginger root
- 3 garlic cloves, finely chopped
- 1/2 cup ground almonds
- 3 onions, thinly sliced
- 1/2 teaspoon dried red chili peppers
- 2 teaspoons salt
- 1 1/2 cups plus fresh coconut milk, or 3/4 cup coconut cream plus 3/4 cup water

2 hard-boiled eggs, chopped

2 cups dried bread cubes

1/2 cup sake

Reserve the duck giblets. Wash and dry the duck, remove all the fat you can, and set aside. Grind the coriander, cumin, saffron, anise, ginger, onions, garlic, and almonds. Mix with the sliced onions, chili peppers, salt, and coconut milk and cook in a saucepan over low heat. Grind the giblets, add the hard-boiled eggs, and add to the cooked stuffing mixture. Toss the bread cubes in the sake, add to the stuffing mixture, and fill the cavity of the bird. (If the stuffing seems too dry, use a little more coconut milk to soften it before stuffing the duck.) Rub the bird with coconut milk and bake it in a roasting pan at 425° for 2 1/2 hours, or until the duck becomes tender and is done.

Serves 4

Variation: Curry Ducky. Omit the almonds, coriander, cumin, and anise, and instead add 1 teaspoon mild curry powder.

FISH AND SHELLFISH

COURT BOUILLON

- 1 bay leaf
- 1 thyme sprig, fresh or dried
- 10 to 12 parsley sprigs
- 1 small onion, sliced
- 6 peppercorns
- 1 cup dry white wine, or 1/4 cup lemon juice, or 1/3 cup vinegar
- 1 quart water
- 1 small carrot, sliced
- 1 teaspoon salt

Tie together the bay leaf, thyme, and parsley to make a bouquet garni. Combine all of the ingredients in a nonaluminum saucepan and simmer for 20 to 30 minutes. Strain, and use to poach seafood.

Makes 1 quart

JAPANESE BAKED FISH

- 4 whole trout, cleaned and gutted
- Juice of 4 lemons
- 8 bacon slices, rendered and fat reserved
- 16 large leaves Savoy cabbage
- 4 large mushrooms, sliced
- 8 pieces candied ginger, sliced
- 4 teaspoons soy sauce
- Large pinch of ground anise seed
- 4 lemons, sliced
- Cornstarch dissolved in cold water
- Salt
- White pepper

Wash the fish, pat dry, and rub with lemon juice. Make shallow incisions at an angle across one side (to be the top) of the fish, such as you see on French breads. Grease a large baking pan with bacon fat, line it with the cabbage leaves, and place the fish on the leaves. Put mushroom and ginger slices in the fish cavities. Sprinkle the fish with soy sauce and anise. Lay slices of lemon on the fish, and bake at 350° for 30 minutes, basting with the pan drippings. Remove the fish from the pan and cover with the cabbage. Strain the liquid from pan and thicken slightly with a bit of cornstarch paste. Season the sauce to taste and serve it on the side.

Serves 4

SAUTÉED BROOK TROUT

- 4 trout, cleaned and gutted
- Butter
- 2 shallots, chopped
- 2 garlic cloves
- 12 small shrimp, peeled and deveined
- 12 small shucked oysters, with their liquor
- 4 jiggers dry or semidry sherry
- Juice of 1 lemon
- 2 large pinches Paul Prudhomme's Seafood Magic Seasoning

In a very large skillet, cook the trout in butter. Set aside. Sauté the shallots, then add the garlic and cook briefly. Add the shrimp, then the oysters and their liquor. Cook for just a few moments, then add the wine, lemon juice, and seafood seasoning. Serve the sauce under the trout on dinner plates.

Serves 4

Note: I have often been asked what I consider the best way to cook fish and why. I have eaten fish prepared in every possible manner and can honestly say that the best piece of fish I ever ate was cooked in an iron skillet in a hobo camp back in the thirties. It was simply sautéed, covered with lemon juice and wine and a bit of onion—and that was it.

BAKED FISH WITH CRAB MEAT STUFFING

- 1 cup crumbs from day-old bread
- 2 tablespoons butter
- 1 rounded tablespoon minced fresh parsley
- 1/2 teaspoon plus salt
- Pepper
- 1/3 cup crab meat
- 1 1/2 tablespoons mixed lemon juice and dry white wine
- 1 3-pound sheepshead (porgy), cleaned
- Flour
- Melted butter

Moisten the bread crumbs with cold water. Gently squeeze out any excess, but do not mash them into a paste. Melt butter in a small heavy skillet and fry the crumbs over low but moderate heat for 3 to 4 minutes, adding more butter as the butter in the skillet is absorbed. Add the parsley and 1/2 teaspoon salt, toss, and add pepper to taste. Add the crab meat and lemon juice and wine. Fill the fish cavity and sew up the ventral slit or fasten with toothpicks. Dredge the fish in flour seasoned with salt and pepper. Shake off any excess. Place in a buttered baking dish, add water just to cover the bottom of the pan, and bake at 400° for 45 to 50 minutes, allowing 16 minutes per pound. Every 10 to 15 minutes, baste with the pan juices and melted butter.

Serve with boiled potatoes, buttered and sprinkled with chopped parsley. On the side, serve a sauceboat with lemon butter (melted butter with lemon juice added). Brown butter or even anchovy butter may also be served with it.

Serves 4 or 5

POACHED WHOLE SALMON

- 3 cups dry white wine
- 3 cups court bouillon (page 92)
- 3 tablespoons black peppercorns
- 3 lemons, sliced
- 2 cups sliced mirepoix (equal parts onion, celery, and carrots)
- 1 bunch parsley
- 1 4- to 6-pound salmon, gutted and scaled

Put all of the ingredients, except the salmon, in a poacher with 3-inch-high sides and bring to a boil. Reduce the heat to a simmer, place the salmon over the liquid, and lightly poach until done, approximately 45 minutes. Do not boil it. Serve hot, or let the fish cool in the liquid, then remove to a platter.

Serves 4

BROILED SWORDFISH WITH LEMON BUTTER

- 4 swordfish steaks (about 8 ounces each)
- 8 tablespoons melted butter (1 stick)
- Juice of 1 whole lemon
- 4 tablespoons dry white wine
- 8 lemon slices

Brush the steaks with melted butter, pour a bit of lemon juice on them, and broil them about 4 inches from the flame of the broiler; turn them once and repeat the process. Mix the wine and remaining butter and lemon juice. When the fish is nearly done, place 2 slices of lemon on each steak and broil to finish. Set the steaks on a large platter, pour on the sauce, and serve.

Serves 4

SALMON STEAKS WITH DILL BUTTER

- 8 tablespoons (1 stick) butter, softened
- Salt
- Pepper
- 4 tablespoons chopped fresh dill
- 2 tablespoons lemon juice
- 4 salmon steaks (1½ inches thick)

Combine the butter, salt, pepper, dill, and lemon juice. Place the salmon steaks in a buttered pan and cover with dill butter. Bake in a preheated 375° to 400° oven for 12 to 14 minutes (or broil for 4 to 6 minutes, turning once), until the center bone is easily removed, approximately 12 minutes.

Serves 4

POACHED SALMON FILLETS WITH McDOLE'S MUSHROOM CREAM SAUCE

- 4 6-ounce salmon fillets
- 1 teaspoon finely chopped shallots
- 2 cups dry white wine
- 2 tablespoons Dijon mustard
- 2 cups sliced mushrooms
- 1 cup heavy cream
- 2 tablespoons finely chopped fresh parsley

Lightly poach the fillets with shallots and wine. Remove the fillets to a warm oven. Add mustard to the pan and reduce until almost dry. Add the mushrooms and cream and reduce to the desired thickness. Add the parsley and pour over the fillets.

Serves 4

SAUTÉED SOLE WITH DILLY SAUCE SUZANNE

- 4 sole fillets
- 2 celery stalks, finely diced
- 1 carrot, finely diced
- 1/4 cup Chablis
- 1 teaspoon Paul Prudhomme's Seafood Magic Seasoning
- 2 tablespoons lemon juice
- 1/2 cup heavy cream
- 4 dill sprigs, finely chopped

Sauté the sole and remove it to a warm holding area. Sauté the celery, carrot, wine, seafood seasoning, and lemon juice. Add the cream and dill, reduce by half, and serve over the fillets.

Serves 4

FRIED FISH FILLETS

- 2 eggs, lightly beaten
- 1 cup flour
- 2 cups dry bread crumbs, seasoned with salt and pepper
- 4 fish fillets
- Mixture of oil and butter

Wash the fish fillets and pat dry. Powder them with flour and dip in egg wash, then bread crumbs. Heat a skillet, add the mixture of oil and butter, and sauté the fish fillets until golden brown. Serve with lemon wedges and/or tartar sauce.

Serves 4

Variation: Use the beer batter on page 6.

LOBSTER SAVANNAH

- 2 large lobsters (2 to 3 pounds each)
- 2 cups plus Newburg sauce (page 243)
- 4 very large shrimp
- 4 very large oysters
- Meat from 4 Alaskan king crab meat legs
- 1 cup crab meat stuffing (page 10; see note below)
- 1 cup hollandaise sauce (page 245)

Cook the lobsters until they turn red. Cut them open from the top, remove the stomachs and intestinal veins and discard. Remove the meat from the tails and claws. Heat the Newburg sauce, add the shrimp, cook slightly, add the oysters, cook slightly, then add the crab meat and lobster meat. Do not let the sauce come to a boil at any time, and be certain that it is very thick, so it will not run out of the lobster shells. Fill the lobster cavities with the sauced meat, then top with crab meat dressing. Place in a 375° oven and heat until the inside is hot. Remove from the oven and pour hollandaise sauce over the crab meat dressing. Set under a broiler until it becomes a light golden color and bubbly. Place each lobster on a large platter and serve. Each is meant to serve two people.

Serves 4

Note: Make the crab meat stuffing using less butter than called for; it should be on the dry side.

CRAB FARCI

- 2 cups crab meat
- 1 stick (8 tablespoons) plus butter
- 1/4 cup slivered scallions, with part of the green
- 1/2 cup soft white bread crumbs
- Juice of 1/2 lemon, strained
- 2 hard-boiled eggs
- Salt
- Cayenne pepper
- 1 rounded tablespoon minced fresh parsley
- Fine dry bread crumbs
- Lemon wedges

Pick over the crab meat carefully and set aside. Melt the cup of butter in a skillet and sauté the scallions for 2 minutes over moderate heat. Add the crab meat and cook for 2 minutes. Add the soft bread crumbs and toss lightly; cook for 2 to 3 minutes, stirring constantly. Remove from the heat. Mix the lemon juice with enough cold water to make 3 tablespoons and dribble over the crab meat mixture. Toss again. Sieve in the hard-cooked egg yolks and toss. Finely chop the egg whites and toss them with the mixture. Add salt and cayenne to taste and the minced parsley. Toss once more. Pile it into buttered crab shells or ramekins and top with fine dry crumbs. Dot with additional butter and bake at 350° until brown, about 20 minutes. Serve with lemon wedges.

Serves 6 to 8

Variation: In New Orleans the soft bread crumbs were first moistened with cold milk, then gently squeezed dry, combined with sautéed chopped onion and garlic, and seasoned with bay leaf, thyme, and parsley. When this mixture was added to the crab meat, it gave the finished dish a moister, almost sauced consistency.

FROG LEGS CREOLE

14 pairs large frog legs
Juice of 1/2 lemon
Salt
Pepper
2 eggs, well beaten
Fine dry bread crumbs
Deep fat for frying
Onion cream sauce (page 244)

Scald the frog legs in a large pot of boiling water with the lemon juice, salt, and pepper. Drain them and pat dry. Dip the legs in egg wash and then in bread crumbs. Fry them in deep fat at 375° for 2 to 3 minutes, or until tender. Serve on a bed of onion cream sauce.

Serves 7

CRAWGATOR STEW

2 sticks (1 cup) butter
1 cup flour
2 quarts chicken stock
1/2 cup chopped onions
3 to 4 tablespoons olive oil
4 garlic cloves
1 6-ounce can tomato paste
1 1-pound can tomatoes
2 pounds alligator meat, cut into bite-size pieces
1/2 cup chopped celery
3 cups diced potatoes
Several large pinches of Paul Prudhomme's Seafood Magic Seasoning
1/2 cup chopped fresh parsley
2 pounds fresh crawfish

In a very large pot, melt the butter and cook the flour slowly in it for a dark brown roux (you must cook it slowly, stirring often in order not to burn it). Slowly add the chicken stock, which will thicken from the roux. In another pot, sauté the onions in olive oil until translucent. Add the garlic, brown it slightly, and discard it. Add the tomato paste and an equal amount of water. Bring to a boil and simmer for 10 minutes.

Add the can of tomatoes and their juice. Cook for a short time, then add the alligator meat. Cook for at least 1 hour.

Add the celery and potatoes. Cook until just done, then add the seafood seasoning and parsley. Turn off the heat and let it marinate overnight in the refrigerator.

Reheat the contents, add the crawfish, cook through and turn the heat off again for another hour or so. Reheat and serve.

Serves 6

This recipe was a gift from my students at Delgado Community College in New Orleans at their graduation buffet. It is original—real Cajun-Creole—and typical of that great city's authentic style of cooking.

DUNBAR'S JAMBALAYA

- 3 tablespoons butter
- 1 small onion, minced
- 1 garlic clove
- 1 1/2 pounds shrimp, peeled and deveined
- 3 small pork sausages or Cajun andouille
- 1/4 pound cooked ham
- 1 tablespoon flour
- 1 6-ounce can tomato paste
- 4 parsley sprigs, minced
- 2 thyme sprigs, minced
- 2 cups hot water
- Salt
- Pepper
- 1/3 cup raw rice

Melt 1 tablespoon butter and brown the onion and garlic. If the shrimp are very large, cut them in half lengthwise. Add the shrimp and cook, stirring, for about 5 minutes, until they are bright pink. Cut the sausages into small pieces and brown in another pan. Cut the ham into cubes the same size as the sausages and sauté with the sausages for a few minutes. Blend in the flour. Combine the meat with the shrimp and add the tomato paste, parsley, and thyme. Add the hot water and bring to a boil. Add salt and pepper to taste, cover, and simmer for 1 hour. Cook the rice according to the directions on the package until it is barely tender. Stir it into the meat mixture and add the remaining butter. Set the pan in a larger pan of hot water

and continue to cook for about 30 minutes, or until the rice has absorbed all the liquid and the mixture is quite dry.
Serves 6

OYSTER AND SHRIMP JAMBALAYA

2 tablespoons olive oil
1 pint shucked oysters
2 onions, chopped
1 garlic clove, pressed
1 small green pepper, seeded and minced
1 pound shrimp, peeled and deveined
1 cup raw rice
2 cups (one 1-pound can) tomatoes
2 cups chicken bouillon or water
1 bay leaf
Pinch of ground thyme
1 teaspoon salt
1/8 teaspoon pepper
1 teaspoon sugar
Minced fresh parsley

Heat the olive oil in a large skillet. Add the oysters and cook over low heat until the edges begin to curl. Remove them from the pan and refrigerate. Cook the onions, garlic, and green pepper in the skillet for 2 to 3 minutes. Add the shrimp and cook until they turn pink; remove them from the pan. Put the rice in the skillet and cook, stirring constantly, until it turns brown. Add the tomatoes, bouillon, and seasonings. Cover and simmer over low heat until the rice is tender and the liquid has been absorbed. Add the oysters and shrimp, heat through, stirring gently, and serve garnished with parsley.
Serves 6

SALMON CAKES

1 egg, beaten
1/2 cup heavy cream
Salt
Pepper
1 tablespoon chopped fresh dill
2 tablespoons finely minced onion
1 tablespoon lemon juice

1 pound cooked salmon, boned and crumbled

2 tablespoons crushed club crackers

Oil

Combine the egg, cream, salt, pepper, dill, onion, and lemon juice. Add the salmon and cracker crumbs. Form into patties and fry in oil until browned and heated through, approximately 4 minutes on each side.

Serves 4

CASSEROLES

So much can be said for casseroles because of their versatility. They can be prepared a great deal ahead of time, frozen, and served at your convenience. Make them as you like, with anything you like.

VEAL-ARTICHOKE DELICIOSO

- 1/2 cup flour mixed with salt and pepper to taste
- 2 pounds stew veal, cut into bite-size pieces
- 4 tablespoons olive oil
- 4 tablespoons butter
- 2 cups finely chopped tomatoes
- 7 or 8 pearl onions
- 3 shallots, finely chopped
- 2 pinches marjoram
- 1 cup veal or chicken stock
- 2 pinches of thyme
- 1 14-ounce can artichoke hearts
- 2 hard-boiled eggs, sliced

Flour the meat. In a casserole large enough to hold all of the ingredients, brown the meat in a mixture of oil and butter. Add all of the remaining ingredients, except the artichokes and eggs, cover the casserole, and bake at 325° for 15 minutes. Stir in the artichokes and cook, covered, for another 15 minutes. Remove from the oven and garnish with egg slices.

Serves 4

OYSTER AND ARTICHOKE CASSEROLE

- 40 shucked oysters
- 2 cups oyster liquor
- 2 bay leaves
- 1/4 teaspoon thyme
- 4 tablespoons roux (flour and butter, cooked)
- 2 cups coarsely chopped scallions
- 12 artichoke hearts, quartered
- Salt
- Pepper
- 4 teaspoons butter
- 1/2 cup bread crumbs
- 1/2 cup grated Parmesan cheese

In a skillet, poach the oysters in the oyster liquor, bay leaves, and thyme until the edges start to curl. Remove them to ramekins. Reduce the oyster liquor to about 1½ cups, add the roux, and blend thoroughly. Add the scallions, artichokes, salt, and pepper. Cook over low heat for about 1 minute. Remove from the heat and add the butter. Spoon the sauce over the oysters. Mix the bread crumbs and Parmesan and sprinkle over the sauce. Bake in a preheated 350° oven for about 10 minutes, until the top is golden brown. Serve immediately, with French bread.

Serves 4

CIOPPINO

- 1 large onion, finely chopped
- Butter
- 2 garlic cloves, minced
- 2 cups fish stock
- 1 1-pound 10-ounce can crushed tomatoes
- 2 celery stalks, finely chopped
- 2 carrots, finely grated
- 2 pinches of Paul Prudhomme's Seafood Magic Seasoning
- 2 pinches of oregano
- Pinch of dry mustard
- Salt
- White pepper
- ½ pound each shrimp, scallops, oysters, king crab meat, and haddock
- 4 ounces Romano cheese, grated

In a casserole, sauté the onions in butter until golden brown. Add the garlic and do the same. Add the fish stock, tomatoes, celery, carrots, and all of the seasonings. Simmer for about 1 hour. Add the scallops and cook for 2 minutes. Add the shrimp and cook for another 2 minutes. Add the oysters and cook for yet another 2 minutes. Add the crab meat, turn off the heat, and let sit. Cut the haddock into bite-size pieces, sauté in butter in another pan, then add to the casserole. Sprinkle on the cheese and bake, uncovered, until the cheese takes on a very light golden brown color.

Serves 6

AMERICAN INDIAN VEGETABLE CASSEROLE

- 4 scallions, finely chopped
- 1 garlic clove, minced
- 1/4 cup salad oil
- 1 zucchini, sliced
- 1 yellow squash, sliced
- 1 eggplant, sliced
- 1 cucumber, seeded and sliced
- 3 tomatoes, diced
- 1 red pepper, seeded and sliced
- 1 green pepper, seeded and sliced
- 1 teaspoon salt
- 1/8 teaspoon each pepper, oregano, cumin, and coriander seed

In a large saucepan, sauté the scallions and garlic in oil until lightly browned. Mix with all of the remaining ingredients, place in a large casserole dish, cover, and bake at 360° for at least 1/2 hour. Remove the cover, turn the heat down to 325°, and let sit for 15 minutes. Check for doneness.

Serves 6

PORK CHOP CASSEROLE

- 2 tablespoons olive oil
- 2 tablespoons butter
- 2 small onions
- 8 pork chops
- 1/2 small can button mushrooms
- 1 celery stalk, cut into 1-inch pieces
- 1 1-pound can tomatoes, chopped
- 1 apple, cored and sliced
- 2 tablespoons flour
- 1 pint pork stock
- 1/2 cup apple cider
- 1/2 tablespoon thyme
- Salt
- Pepper
- 2 tablespoons currant jelly

Heat the oil and butter in a very large casserole. Chop the onions and sauté them in the mixture until golden brown. Fry the pork chops in this until browned on both sides. Mix in the rest of the vegetables and the apple and cook. Stir in the flour and cook for 4 to 5 minutes. Add the stock, cider, and thyme, and season to your taste. Add the currant jelly and stir well. Cover and bake at 325° for 1 hour.

Serves 4

PORK, POTATOES, AND SAUERKRAUT

- 4 large pork cutlets or 8 chops
- 8 potatoes, unpeeled
- 1 1-pound 10-ounce can sauerkraut
- 2 teaspoons caraway seeds
- Large dash of powdered coriander seeds
- Salt
- Pepper
- 2 tablespoons vodka
- Butter

Cook the pork and set aside. Slice the potatoes and cook them until almost done. Season the sauerkraut with the caraway seeds, coriander seeds, salt, pepper, and vodka. Butter the bottom of a casserole dish. Put a layer of potatoes on the bottom and top it with the pork, sauerkraut, and another layer of potatoes. Dot the top with butter. Bake at 375° for as long as it takes for the top and bottom layers to cook through. Test with a toothpick or fork to see if the potatoes are soft.

Serves 4

LAMB CASSEROLE

- 3 large potatoes, thinly sliced
- 2 large zucchini, thinly sliced
- 1 onion, finely chopped
- Butter
- 3 eggs
- 1/2 cup Italian-flavored bread crumbs
- 1/2 cup grated Romano cheese
- 3 cups diced cooked lamb
- 2 large tomatoes

Cook the potatoes and zucchini. Sauté the onion in a bit of butter. Set aside. Beat the eggs until foamy. Mix the bread crumbs and Romano cheese. Butter a large casserole dish. Place a layer of potatoes on the bottom. Sprinkle a bit bread crumb mixture on it, and top with some of the lamb, then tomatoes, then zucchini. Pour half the beaten eggs over this. Repeat the process again. Top the whole thing with bread crumb mixture and bake, covered, in a preheated 360° oven for 15 minutes. Remove the cover and bake until the top turns slightly brown.

Serves 6

If you have lamb left over from a previous meal, try this.

BAKED MACARONI, SAUSAGE, CHEESE, AND TOMATOES

- 1 pound breakfast-type link sausage
- 1 pound plus 6 slices American or cheddar cheese
- 1 pound macaroni
- 1 1-pound 12-ounce can tomatoes
- Salt
- Pepper

Cook the sausage and save the drippings. Chop the pound of cheese. Cook the macaroni until *al dente* and drain. In a large mixing bowl, mix the sausage drippings with the tomatoes, chopped cheese, and hot macaroni. Season with salt and pepper. Pour into a 3- to 4-quart casserole with a cover. Mix in the sausage, either whole or cut into bite-size pieces. Pour it all into the casserole dish, top with the 6 slices of cheese, and bake, covered, in a preheated 350° oven for about 15 minutes. Uncover and let it sit in the oven just until the cheese is a nice golden brown.

Serves 4

CAJUN ANDOUILLE, RED BEANS, AND RICE

- 2 ham hocks
- 1 pound dried red kidney beans
- 2 cups chopped celery
- 1 cup chopped green peppers

- 1/2 teaspoon garlic powder
- 1 teaspoon Cajun seasoning
- 1 teaspoon Tabasco sauce
- 1 cup finely chopped onions
- 2 bay leaves
- 1 teaspoon oregano
- 1/2 teaspoon pepper
- 1 pound andouille sausage
- 4 cups hot cooked rice

Cook the ham hocks in water to make stock; remove the hocks and reserve. Cook the beans, with the next nine ingredients, in the stock. Stir the pot often so the beans will not stick. Halfway through the cooking, add the sausage. The dish is done when the beans are very soft and falling apart. Place the rice in the center of a platter, surround it with the bean mixture, and put the ham hocks at one end and sausage at the other.

Serves 6

KNACKWURST, SAUERKRAUT, AND POTATO CASSEROLE

- 1 2-pound package sauerkraut, drained, juice reserved
- 1 cup flat beer
- 2 tablespoons caraway seeds
- 1 large onion, chopped
- Butter
- 1 large apple
- 4 links knackwurst (or bratwurst)
- Pepper
- 6 potatoes, peeled and thinly sliced

Heat the sauerkraut in the beer; drain and season with caraway seeds. Sauté the onion in butter and add it to the sauerkraut. Core and chop the apple and set aside. Heat the sausage in the sauerkraut juice and pepper. Place a layer of half the potatoes in the bottom of a casserole dish, put the sausage on it, top with the sauerkraut, and sprinkle the chopped apple on that. Top with another layer of potatoes. Pour the sauerkraut juice over all and bake, covered, at 350° until you see a great deal of bubbling in the casserole dish. Check the potatoes for doneness with a toothpick, and if they are done, leave the cover off and bake until they reach a nice rich golden brown.

Serves 4

KIELBASA, PULATSKIS, AND CABBAGE CASSEROLE

1	large link kielbasa (Polish sausage)		Salt
			Pepper
1/2	large head cabbage	2	potatoes
4	slices bacon	1/2	large onion, chopped
1	tablespoon caraway seeds	1	egg
		1/4	cup plus flour

Cook the kielbasa till just slightly crisp. Chop the cabbage into bite-size pieces. Chop the bacon the same way. Fry the bacon to crispness. Remove from the pan, reserve, and sauté the cabbage in the bacon fat. Season with caraway seeds and salt and pepper. Return the bacon to the pan.

To make the pulatskis (potato pancakes), peel and slice the potatoes; put them in a food processor, add the onion, egg, and flour, and blend together. If the mixture is too thin, add flour; if too thick, add a bit of milk. Shape into 3 pancakes, each the size of the casserole dish. In a skillet, cook the pancakes till just slightly browned on both sides.

Cut the sausage into lengthwise slices. Put a pancake on the bottom of the casserole dish, then a layer of sausage and a layer of cabbage; top with another pancake and repeat the process. Cover the casserole dish and bake at 350° for 10 minutes. Take the cover off and just slightly dry the top, then serve.

Serves 4

CANADIAN BOUDOIN SAUSAGE CASSEROLE

- 1 large boudoin (blood sausage)
- 6 large potatoes
- Butter
- Milk
- Salt
- Pepper
- 1 small onion, finely minced
- 4 large carrots

Cook the boudoin until the skin just begins to crack. Set aside. Peel, cut up, and cook the potatoes. Mash them with butter, milk, salt, and pepper, and whip in the onion. Peel the carrots and cut them into uniform lengthwise slices. Cook them until just done.

Butter the bottom and sides of a large casserole dish. Place a layer of mashed potatoes on the bottom. Place a layer of the sausage on this, and a layer of the carrots on that. Top with the remainder of the sausage and another layer of mashed potatoes, and dot the top with bits of butter. Bake, covered, in a preheated 350° oven for 20 minutes. Uncover, brown slightly, and serve.

Serves 4

VEGETABLES

*V*egetables are the real mainstay in our food chain. Without them we would never be able to keep ourselves well. There's no getting away from it.

Vegetables should be eaten raw as often as possible. If you must cook them, do it rapidly, in as short a time as possible. The longer you cook, the less you will garner in the way of nutriments. The Chinese method of cooking is still the best when it comes to retaining most of the vegetables' goodness; they do not cook their vegetables to death. A large skillet is no different from a wok, and in it you can sauté as well as any Chinese chef.

GREEN BEANS AND CHEESE

- 4 cups cooked green beans
- 1/4 teaspoon salt
- 1/8 teaspoon pepper
- 1 1/2 cups grated cheese
- 2 tablespoons butter
- 1/3 cup heavy cream

Put the beans in a buttered baking dish and season with salt and pepper. Add 1/2 cup of the cheese, 1 tablespoon butter, and the cream. Stir until mixed. Sprinkle on with the remaining cheese and dot with the remaining butter. Bake in a preheated 325° oven for about 20 minutes.

Serves 4

BAKED LIMA BEANS

- 5 tablespoons plus butter
- 3 tablespoons flour
- 1 1/4 cups milk
- 3 1/2 cups cooked lima beans
- 1/2 teaspoon salt
- 1/8 teaspoon pepper
- 2 eggs, well beaten
- 1/2 cup bread crumbs

Melt the 5 tablespoons butter, blend in the flour, add the milk, stir, and cook until thickened. Press the beans through a sieve and combine with the sauce. Add the salt, pepper, and eggs. Pour into a buttered baking dish, cover with the bread crumbs, dot with butter, and bake in a preheated 375° oven for about 20 minutes.

Serves 4

RED BEANS AND RICE

- 1/2 pound lean salt pork, diced
- 1 garlic clove, minced
- 2 1/2 cups (1 1-pound 5-ounce can) red kidney beans, drained
- 3 cups cooked rice
- Minced fresh parsley
- Salt
- Pepper

Fry the salt pork until crisp and brown. Remove the pork and reserve; pour off half the fat. Add the garlic to the skillet and cook for 2 to 3 minutes. Add the beans, rice, parsley, and salt and pepper to taste. Heat through. Serve topped with salt pork.

Serves 4

CREOLE WAX BEANS

- 1/4 cup chopped onions
- 1/4 cup diced green pepper
- 3 tablespoons butter
- 1 1/2 tablespoons flour
- 1 1/2 cups tomato juice
- 1/4 teaspoon salt
- 1/8 teaspoon pepper
- 3 cups cooked wax beans

Cook the onions and green pepper in the butter until the onions are yellow. Blend in the flour, add the tomato juice, and simmer for 5 minutes. Add the salt, pepper, and beans and heat through. Serve hot.

Serves 4

ROSEBUD BEETS AND PINEAPPLE

- 3/4 cup sugar
- 2 tablespoons cornstarch
- 1/3 cup vinegar
- 1/3 cup water
- 4 cups cooked whole small beets
- 1 cup pineapple chunks
- Salt
- Pepper
- 3 tablespoons butter

Combine the sugar and cornstarch; add the vinegar and water. Cook over low heat until thickened and clear; do not boil hard. Add the beets and simmer for 5 minutes. Add the pineapple and heat well. Add the salt, pepper, and butter, heat, and serve.

Serves 4

LADY CABBAGE

- 1 medium head new cabbage
- 1 1/2 teaspoons salt
- 3 tablespoons butter
- 1/8 teaspoon pepper

Bring 1 quart water to a boil in a 3-quart saucepan. Put the cabbage and salt in the boiling water. Bring the water back to a boil and cook the cabbage for 2 minutes. Turn off the heat and let the cabbage stand in the water until tender and light green. Drain the cabbage and add the butter and pepper. Serve hot.

Serves 4

Variation: Chop the cabbage and cook it in bacon fat. Add 1 tablespoon caraway seeds and 6 slices of bacon, cooked and crumbled.

CARROT MOLD

- 2 cups mashed cooked carrots
- Sugar
- 2 eggs, well beaten
- 1/2 cup heavy cream
- 1/2 teaspoon salt
- 1/4 teaspoon white pepper
- 1 pinch of nutmeg

Scrape the carrots and slice or halve them. Cook in lightly sweetened water, about 1 tablespoon sugar per quart of water, until tender. Drain and mash them. Measure out 4 cups. Combine the carrots and eggs and then beat with the cream and seasonings. Turn into a buttered ring mold, set the mold in a pan of hot water, and bake in a preheated 375° oven for 30 minutes, or until set. Unmold on a heated serving dish. If you wish, fill the center with some other vegetable; peas, lima beans, or the like would do fine.

Serves 12

Carrots, which came into favor in the early eighteenth century, were nothing to speak of as a general rule save for their flavor when added to soups or stews. You could find them in Indian cooking in this country, for they were much used by them, but the Cajuns did get around to using them in many ways soon after they came here, and eventually carrots became very popular. This dish is from the early eighteenth century.

CAULIFLOWER POLONAISE

- 1 large head cauliflower
- 8 tablespoons (1 stick) butter
- 1/4 pound grated Romano cheese
- 1/2 cup seasoned bread crumbs
- Juice of 1 lemon
- 1/4 cup dry sauterne
- Salt
- Pepper
- Paprika

Blanch the cauliflower and cut up into small florets. Melt the butter in a skillet and sauté them. As soon as they begin to color slightly, add the cheese, bread crumbs, lemon juice, and wine. Stir with a wooden spoon and turn the florets over and over until they begin to become coated with the ingredients. Season to taste.

Serves 6

CORN PO

- 3 cups mashed potatoes (see note)
- 3 tablespoons melted butter
- Salt
- Pepper
- 1/2 cup milk or half-and-half
- 1 cup whole-kernel corn, drained
- Vegetable oil
- Maple syrup

Combine the potatoes, melted butter, salt, pepper, milk, and corn. Form pancake-size patties and fry in oil until golden brown. Serve with maple syrup.

Serves 4

Note: If you are using leftover mashed potatoes, do not add butter, milk, salt, or pepper.

FRENCH-STYLE PEAS

- 3 tablespoons butter
- 1/4 cup lean salt pork, diced and blanched
- 1 head romaine lettuce, shredded
- 1 medium onion, finely diced
- 2 cups green peas
- 1 teaspoon sugar
- 2 parsley sprigs
- 1/4 cup chicken stock
- Large pinch of thyme
- Salt
- Pepper

Heat the butter in a saucepan, add the salt pork, and sauté, stirring often, for 10 minutes. Add the lettuce and sauté for another 5 minutes. Add the remaining ingredients, cover the pan, and simmer for 5 minutes. Uncover and cook until all the liquid has evaporated and the onions and peas are just done.

Serves 6

CREOLE BLACK-EYED PEAS

- 1/2 pound dried black-eyed peas
- 1 dried hot red pepper
- 1/4 cup mixed chopped red and green peppers
- Butter
- Salt
- Pepper
- 1/2 small onion, sliced into rings

In a pot, cover the peas with 3 cups cold water. Bring to a boil and boil for 2 minutes. Set aside and let stand for at least 1 hour. Add the dried pepper, bring to a boil, and simmer, covered, for 30 minutes, or until the peas are tender, adding more water if necessary. Stir in the chopped peppers and cook for a few minutes. Season to taste with butter, salt, and pepper. Sauté the onion rings slightly in butter, then serve them on top as a garnish.

Serves 6

BAKED STUFFED POTATOES

- 2 Idaho baking potatoes
- 4 tablespoons butter
- 1/4 pound cheddar cheese, grated
- Salt
- Pepper
- 1/4 cup milk or half-and-half
- 1/4 pound bacon, cooked and crumbled
- Melted butter

Bake the potatoes in a 400° oven until firm but done. Let cool. Slice the potatoes in half lengthwise, or cut off the top third. Scoop out almost all of the pulp in both parts. Combine it with the butter, cheese, salt, pepper, and milk. Mash. Mix in the bacon and stuff the potato skins. Drizzle with melted butter and bake at 375° until golden brown.

Serves 4

Variations: Omit the bacon and add half a Spanish onion, diced and sautéed, and 1/2 tablespoon paprika; or 1/4 pound diced cooked chicken; or 1/4 pound cooked sausage meat.

SPANISH FRIES

- Oil
- 1 green pepper, seeded and sliced
- 1 red pepper, seeded and sliced
- 1 medium onion, sliced
- 4 large potatoes, peeled, cubed, and blanched
- 1 tablespoon capers
- 6 green olives, sliced
- 6 black olives, sliced
- Salt
- Pepper

Heat oil in a skillet. Sauté the green and red peppers and onion for 2 minutes. Add the potatoes and sauté until they are golden brown. Add the capers, olives, salt, and pepper. Toss and serve.

Serves 4

JEWISH POTATO KNISHES

Filling

- 2 medium potatoes
- 2 tablespoons oil
- 1 small onion, finely chopped
- 1/2 teaspoon salt
- 1/4 teaspoon pepper
- 1 small egg

Dough

- 1 cup sifted flour
- 1/4 teaspoon salt
- 1/2 teaspoon baking powder
- 1 egg
- 1/4 cup oil
- 1 1/2 tablespoons ice water

Scrub the potatoes. Put in a pot with water to cover, bring to a boil, then turn the heat down to medium, cover, and cook until soft, about 30 minutes. Pour off the cooking water and pour cold water over the potatoes to cool them. Peel and mash. Heat the oil in a skillet and cook the onion over medium heat until golden brown. Add to the mashed potatoes, along with the salt, pepper, and egg. Mix well and set aside. Put the flour, salt, and baking powder in a bowl. Mix well with a spoon, about 35 to 40 strokes. Add the egg, oil, and ice water. Mix until the dough holds together in a ball. Place the dough on a pastry board and knead until smooth.

Heat the oven to 350°. Butter a cookie sheet.

Divide the dough in half. Dust a rolling pin and half the dough with flour to keep it from sticking. Roll out the dough to a very thin, wide rectangle, about 8 × 12 inches. Brush a few drops of oil on it. Place a strip of the filling, about 1 inch thick, at the top edge of the dough. Roll it up like a jelly roll. Cut the roll into pieces about 2 inches long and put them on the cookie sheet. Repeat with the second piece of dough. Bake for 30 to 35 minutes, until golden brown. Serve the knishes hot, with sour cream. If you must make them ahead of time, reheat them in the oven for about 5 minutes.

Makes 16 to 18

STUFFED SQUASH

- 3 summer squash
- 2 ounces lean cooked ham
- 4 ounces cooked and peeled shrimp
- 1 onion, sliced
- 1/3 cup butter
- 1/2 cup plus stale French bread crumbs
- 1 thyme sprig
- 1 tablespoon chopped fresh parsley
- 1/2 garlic clove, chopped
- Salt
- Pepper
- Pimiento strips
- Parsley sprigs

Wash the squash and cook them in boiling salted water to cover until they are tender enough to be pierced with a skewer. Cut the squash in half and scoop out the pulp, being careful not to break the shells. Reserve the shells. Mash the pulp and put it through a food chopper with the ham, shrimp, and onion. Melt 4 tablespoons butter in a heavy skillet and add the ham mixture. Cook over low heat, stirring occasionally, for 20 minutes. Soak the 1/2 cup bread crumbs in water and press them dry.

Add the crumbs to the skillet, along with the thyme, parsley, and garlic. Season with salt and pepper and toss well to blend. Simmer over low heat for 10 minutes, stirring constantly. Pile the stuffing into the squash shells, mounding it high. Sprinkle with more bread crumbs and dot with the remaining butter. Bake in a preheated 350° oven for about 25 minutes, until the topping is golden brown. Garnish each with a strip of pimiento and a parsley sprig. Serve as a side dish.

Serves 6

This is a Japanese favorite I learned in Kyoto. I even served it to the head of the Sumitomo Corp., in 1985 at the Delta Point River Restaurant.

STUFFED ZUCCHINI

- Large pinch of ground ginger
- 1 teaspoon soy sauce
- 1 slice bread
- 8 ounces mixed leftover meat (beef, veal, bacon, etc.)
- Salt
- Pepper
- 1/2 large onion, finely chopped
- 3 medium-size zucchini
- 1/2 cup canned tomato sauce

Make a stuffing out of all of the ingredients, except the zucchini and tomato sauce. Slice the zucchini in half lengthwise and remove the core. Fill the cavities of the zucchini with stuffing. Lightly butter a baking pan, put the zucchini in it, and bake at 350° for 30 minutes or so, depending on the firmness of the vegetable. Serve with a small amount of tomato sauce on top.

Serves 6

PASTA

The word *pasta* seems to indicate so much that many people become a bit confused by it. The word means "paste," and refers to noodles of various kinds—for example, spaghetti, spaghettini, elbow macaroni, riccolini, amorini, vermicelli, lumache, and lasagna.

The first lesson in pasta is to learn how to cook it properly. Use a great deal of salted water and keep it boiling during the entire cooking process. Never overcook it, for that will indeed turn it to paste; always try to cook it *al dente,* which means cooked yet still firm. Of course, if you are going to recook pasta, as in an oven-baked dish, then you do not cook it nearly as much in the beginning.

RAVIOLI

Dough

- 4 cups sifted flour
- 2 teaspoons salt
- 3 eggs, slightly beaten
- Up to 1/4 cup ice water
- Flour for rolling out

Spinach Filling

- Olive oil
- 1 package frozen spinach, thawed and well drained
- Pepper
- 2 tablespoons chopped fresh parsley
- 2 hard-boiled eggs, grated
- 4 ounces mozzarella cheese

Sift the flour and salt into a mound on a board or counter top. Make a well in the center and put the eggs in the well. Mix together with one hand, adding ice water, a bit at a time, with the other. Add only enough water to make the dough firm. Flour the board and knead the dough until smooth and elastic. Cut into 4 parts. Roll out each until about 1/8 inch thick, or slightly thinner, if you like. Roll each section loosely in floured towels so it does not dry out while you make the filling.

To make the filling, heat the oil in a skillet. Add the spinach, pepper, and parsley. Heat through, remove from the heat, and add the eggs and cheese. Mix together.

Lay out the first sheet of dough and score it into 1 1/2- to 2-inch squares. If you like, paint the score lines with water, egg wash, or milk, using a pastry brush. Put some filling in the center of each square, then top with another sheet of dough. With a knife, slice through the two layers of dough to cut into squares with the filling inside. Press the edges of the squares together or pinch them all down with a fork, to seal them. Repeat with the remaining dough and filling. Boil the ravioli and serve with a sauce.

Serves 4

Variations: Substitute ricotta or cottage cheese in place of the mozzarella. You can also use cooked meat instead of the cheese, and add just a bit of bread crumbs to bind. Or use one of the stuffings for pasta shells.

This dough and the egg noodles that follow can be cut into many types of pasta—lasagna, fettuccine, spaghettini, cannelloni, etc.

EGG NOODLES

4 cups sifted flour
1 teaspoon salt
4 eggs
1 teaspoon vegetable oil

Sift the flour and salt onto a board or counter top. Make a well in the center. Put the eggs and oil in the well and work it with your fingers until a fine dough is formed. Knead for at least 10 to 15 minutes, until very smooth and elastic. Place in a bowl and set to rest for 20 minutes or so. Divide the dough into 3 parts. Roll out and cut into strips for lasagna or other pasta. Cook *al dente.*

Serves 4

POTATO GNOCCHI

2 pounds potatoes
2 egg yolks, beaten
1 1/2 teaspoons salt
About 1 1/2 cups flour
1 to 2 tablespoons melted butter

Cook the potatoes. Let cool, peel them, and dry in a pan on the stove, over low heat. Mash. Mix in the yolks, salt, and enough flour to make dough. Mix in melted butter. Roll out to the thickness of a finger. Cut into small pieces and roll them with your fingers into pieces resembling conch shells. Cook for about 10 minutes. Serve with butter and cheese or with a sauce.

Serves 4

THE STANDARD SPAGHETTI SAUCE

- 1/2 onion, finely minced
- Olive oil
- 2 garlic cloves, finely minced
- 1 12-ounce can tomato paste
- 2 1-lb 14-ounce cans regular or plum tomatoes, crushed or chopped
- 1 large pinch of Italian seasoning
- 1 tablespoon sugar
- Pepper
- 2 jiggers brandy

Sauté the onion in a bit of oil in a large pot. When just done, add the garlic and sauté until lightly golden. Add the tomato paste, plus an equal amount of water, and bring to a boil. Simmer for about 10 minutes, then add the tomatoes. Return it to a boil, then simmer for at least 30 minutes. Add the Italian seasoning, sugar, pepper, and brandy. Cook for about 10 minutes. Check for seasoning. Serve with spaghetti.

Serves 5 or 6

Most people have learned to make spaghetti sauce, but many have difficulty getting the acidity out of it. Some use baking soda, others an overabundance of sugar, still others wine by the cupful. My way, I guarantee no acid!

SPAGHETTI WITH WHITE CLAM SAUCE

- 6 tablespoons olive oil
- 6 garlic cloves, chopped
- 24 to 32 shucked clams, liquor reserved, or 1 medium can
- 2 large pinches of basil
- 2 large pinches of oregano
- Pepper
- Chopped fresh parsley

Heat a large skillet, add the oil, and heat it. Add the garlic and sauté very lightly, not permitting it to turn brown. Add the shucked clams and sauté them for just a few minutes, then add the seasonings, cook a bit, and add the reserved clam liquor. (If the clams are canned, add them and their liquor along with the basil, then the oregano, and finally the pepper.) Serve with a thin-style spaghetti. Top with parsley.

Serves 4

Variation: Spaghetti with Red Clam Sauce. Add a cup of spaghetti sauce.

SPAGHETTI WITH GARLIC AND OIL

- 1½ pounds spaghetti
- ½ cup olive oil
- 1 small onion, finely minced
- 8 plus garlic cloves
- Pepper
- ½ cup finely chopped fresh parsley

Cook the spaghetti and set aside. Keep warm. Heat a skillet, add the oil, and heat it. Add the onion and sauté until clarified. Add the garlic and sauté it to a very light golden color. Add the pepper and parsley, heat through, and serve immediately over the spaghetti.

Serves 6

THE CLASSIC FETTUCCINE ALFREDO

- 1 pound wide fettuccine noodles
- 1 pound Parmesan cheese
- 4 sticks (2 cups) butter, cut into small pieces

Cook the noodles until just done; drain. Add half of the butter and toss to melt it. Grate in half of the cheese and toss all together in a large heatproof bowl. Bake in a preheated 400° oven for 5 minutes. Remove, add the remaining butter, grate in the remaining cheese, and serve, as is. This is the only true fettuccine Alfredo, although today it is often made with cream added.

Serves 4

STUFFED SHELLS THE EASY WAY

- 1 garlic clove, crushed
- Large pasta shells (4 per person)
- 1 1/2 pounds ricotta cheese
- 1/4 cup heavy cream
- 2 tablespoons Italian dry white wine
- 3 eggs, well beaten
- 6 tablespoons chopped fresh parsley
- 6 tablespoons grated Romano cheese
- White pepper

Heat a large pot of water with the garlic in it. Cook the shells only until they become somewhat rubbery, ***not al dente,*** for they will be cooked further in the oven. Mix all of the other ingredients together and use to stuff the shells. Place them in a large oven pan, pour in a little water (or some of the sauce you will be serving), cover the pan, and bake in a preheated 325° oven for 15 minutes. Uncover the pan and give it but 5 minutes more. Serve with sauce—white, cheese, or tomato.

Serves 6 to 8

Variation: Shells with Meat Stuffing.

- 1 cup ground Italian ham
- 1/4 cup ground chicken or veal
- 1/2 teaspoon grated lemon zest
- 1/2 pound ricotta cheese
- 2 eggs, well beaten
- 1/8 teaspoon grated nutmeg
- 1 cup soft bread crumbs
- 2 tablespoons finely chopped fresh parsley

Mix together and use to stuff the shells.

MONTERREY PLAZA'S SAFFRON TAGLIATELLE WITH SHRIMP

- 2 tablespoons shallots
- 1 tablespoon olive oil
- 1 very large tomato, peeled and seeded
- 6 ounces dry white wine
- 4 ounces fish stock
- 12 ounces bay shrimp
- 1 pound saffron-flavored tagliatelle, cooked
- 4 tablespoons butter
- 2 tablespoons chopped fresh parsley
- Salt
- Pepper

Sauté the shallots in oil; add the tomato, wine, and fish stock. Reduce by one half. Add the shrimp and cook until done. Add the tagliatelle and bring to a boil. Remove from the heat and stir in the butter, parsley, and salt and pepper to taste.

Serves 4

I was given this recipe by chef Steve Pagano at the Monterrey Plaza when I was a guest there in 1986. To me, it's one of the classiest luncheon dishes of all time.

VERMICELLI WITH RICOTTA CHEESE

- 1 cup milk
- 1 pound ricotta cheese
- 2 tablespoons butter
- 4 tablespoons grated Parmesan cheese
- Salt
- Pepper
- 1 pound vermicelli

Warm the milk, add the ricotta, and cream them together. Add the butter, half of the Parmesan cheese, and salt and pepper. Cook the vermicelli, then mix with the cheese sauce. Serve with a light sprinkling of the remaining Parmesan cheese.

Serves 4

THREE-CHEESE PASTA

- Italian seasoned bread crumbs
- 1 pound egg noodle bows
- 2 tablespoons butter
- 4 ounces freshly grated Parmesan cheese
- 4 ounces Swiss cheese, chopped
- 4 ounces mozzarella cheese, chopped
- 4 cups béchamel sauce (page 242)

Butter a large casserole dish and sprinkle with bread crumbs. Cook the noodles and toss with the butter and cheeses. Place half of the mixture in the casserole dish and top with half of the béchamel sauce. Put the rest of the mixture in the casserole dish and pour the remaining sauce over it. Top with a light coating of bread crumbs and bake in a preheated 350° oven for 15 to 20 minutes, being careful not to burn the top.

Serves 4

PASTA AND PEAS

- 1 pound curly pasta
- 4 tablespoons olive oil
- 4 garlic cloves, crushed
- 1 1-pound 12-ounce can plum tomatoes, crushed
- Salt
- Pepper
- 1½ cups frozen peas

Cook the pasta *al dente.* Heat the oil in a skillet and sauté the garlic. Add the tomatoes, salt, and pepper. Bring to a boil, turn the heat down to a simmer, add the peas, and heat through. Serve over the pasta. You can serve grated cheese with it, if you like.

Serves 4

Variation: Omit the tomatoes and add 6 mushrooms, chopped, and 6 ounces grated mozzarella cheese.

PASTA WITH MUSHROOMS AND PEAS

- 1 pound thin spaghetti
- 2 to 3 tablespoons olive oil
- 2 to 3 tablespoons bacon fat
- 12 mushrooms, thinly sliced
- 1 10-ounce package frozen peas, thawed
- 8 slices bacon, cooked and crumbled
- Pepper
- 1/2 cup grated Parmesan cheese

Break the spaghetti into 1- to 2-inch pieces. Cook and set aside. Add olive oil to the bacon fat in a skillet, heat, and sauté the mushrooms until cooked. Add the peas and just heat through. Mix in the spaghetti, bacon, and pepper. Serve with a sprinkling of Parmesan cheese.

Serves 4

PASTA PRIMAREDA

Dressing

- 1/2 cup red wine vinegar
- 1 teaspoon minced garlic
- 1 large onion, grated
- 3 tablespoons each chopped fresh sweet basil and dill, or 1 tablespoon each dried
- 1 teaspoon pepper
- 3 tablespoons olive oil
- 1 each green and red pepper, seeded and finely minced
- 1 tablespoon Italian seasoning
- 1 tablespoon ground caraway seeds

1 package rotini noodles (three colors—made with egg, spinach, and carrots)

- 24 to 36 thumb-size florets mixed broccoli and cauliflower
- 1 pound chicken meat, cut into bite-size pieces
- 1 pound very small shrimp, peeled and deveined
- 8 ounces mozzarella cheese, sliced or grated

Put all of the dressing ingredients in a pot, bring to a boil, turn the heat down to a simmer, and cook for just a few minutes. Set aside and keep warm.

Cook the noodles *al dente.* Steam the florets. Sauté the chicken. Cook the shrimp. Mix together with the dressing, add the cheese, and serve.

Serves 4

PASTA PRIMAVEGA

- 1 package curly pasta
- 6 scallions, chopped
- 1 large cucumber, peeled, seeded, and diced
- 1 each green and red pepper, seeded and chopped
- 6 large mushrooms, sliced
- 2 celery stalks, chopped
- 1 red onion, chopped
- 1 yellow onion, chopped
- 2 large carrots, chopped
- 4 radishes, sliced
- 1 large zucchini, diced

Seasoning Mixture

- 4 tablespoons olive oil
- 1 large onion
- 10 tablespoons chopped fresh sweet basil or 4 tablespoons dried
- 1 tablespoon ground coriander
- 1 tablespoon dark soy sauce
- 4 garlic cloves
- 1 tablespoon pepper
- 2 tablespoons rosemary
- 1/2 cup white wine vinegar
- 2 tomatoes, chopped

Cook the pasta and keep warm. Steam the vegetables, starting with the one that takes longest to cook. Cook the seasonings together; add the tomatoes last and just let them warm through. Combine everything in a large mixing bowl and serve.

Serves 4

Note: Instead of the seasoning mixture you can use a packaged seasoning mix. Also, the dish can be served cold, too.

CHICKEN AND PEANUTS WITH LONG-LIFE NOODLES

- 1/4 cup peanut oil
- 1 cup raw peanuts
- 1 pound sliced cooked chicken meat
- 1 can bamboo shoots
- 2 tablespoons dark soy sauce
- 6 scallions, chopped
- 1 can sliced water chestnuts
- 2 tablespoons sherry
- Pepper
- 1 pound egg noodles

Heat the oil in a preheated wok or skillet and cook the peanuts until just slightly browned. Remove and chop. Return them to the pan and add all of the remaining ingredients, except the noodles. Sauté lightly to heat through. Cook the noodles and place on a large serving platter. Cover with the chicken mixture.

Serves 6

There are several types of Chinese noodles, such as cellophane noodles, sometimes called Chinese vermicelli or bean thread; fresh noodles, called lo mein, made with eggs; yee fu noodles, a fried dried egg noodle. At feasts, most dishes are usually served with noodles, often of great length, for the Chinese have always regarded the noodle as a symbol of longevity.

This recipe shows how you can make a large number of dishes from one basic method of preparation. A wok is the ideal utensil, but you can use a large skillet and accomplish the same result.

JAPANESE NOODLES AND PORK IN BROWN SAUCE

- 4 dried mushrooms
- 1½ tablespoons brown bean sauce
- ½ garlic clove, finely minced
- ½ teaspoon sugar
- 1 slice ginger root, finely minced
- 8 ounces ground pork
- ½ tablespoon hoisin sauce
- 2 tablespoons sake
- ½ tablespoon dark soy sauce
- ½ pound fresh noodles
- 1½ tablespoons peanut oil

Soak the mushrooms in water for at least 1 hour, then slice them thin. Mix the bean sauce, garlic, sugar, and ginger, and in another bowl mix the pork, hoisin sauce, sake, and soy sauce. Set aside. Cook the noodles and set aside to keep warm. Heat the oil in a large skillet, add the bean sauce mixture and mushrooms, and stir-fry very quickly. Add the pork mixture and stir-fry until the pork is well cooked. If it seems somewhat dry, add about ¼ cup water, cover the skillet, and cook for another 5 to 6 minutes. Place the noodles on a very large platter and serve the sauced pork over it.

Serves 4

RICE

Rice is one of the most diversified of foods. Although the Far East is supposedly where rice is king, more varieties are grown in this country. The usual basic division is into long-grain and short-grain. Long-grain rice is long and narrow. Short-grain rice is most commonly used by those for whom rice is a mainstay.

BOILED RICE

1 cup raw long-grain rice
2 cups water

Wash the rice under running water until the water runs clear. Put it in a saucepan with the 2 cups water. Cover lightly and bring to a boil over high heat. Reduce the heat to its lowest point and cook for 20 minutes.

Serves 6

GRAHAM KERR'S STEAMED RICE

5/8 cup long-grain rice
3 pints water
1 tablespoon salt

Wash the rice under cold water until no color shows in the runoff. Put the 3 pints water in a pot, add the salt, and bring to a boil. Let the rice fall in a bit at a time; let it boil for 10 minutes. Drain the rice in a metal colander, and set the colander on top of a saucepan with a small amount of water in it. Place a lid over the rice and steam it for 8 minutes. Fluff it up with a fork.

Serves 6 to 8

This is the very best steamed rice I have ever tried, thanks to my good friend Graham Kerr, the former Galloping Gourmet.

INDIAN YELLOW RICE

1 cup raw long-grain rice
3 tablespoons butter
2 1/2 cups chicken stock
1/8 teaspoon powdered saffron

In a 4-quart pot, sauté the rice in butter until it turns a light golden brown. Heat the chicken stock, add the saffron, and add this to the rice. Bring it to a boil again, set on simmer, and cook for about 30 minutes, being certain not to disturb it during that time.

Serves 6

YELLOW RICE PILAF

- 2½ cups chicken stock
- Several drops yellow food coloring
- 1 cup raw rice
- 8 tablespoons (1 stick) butter
- 1 red and 1 green pepper, seeded and coarsely chopped
- 1 large onion, coarsely chopped
- 8 mushrooms, thinly sliced

Heat the chicken stock and add food coloring to make it a very rich yellow. Put in the rice and bring to a boil. Let it boil for 1 minute, then let it simmer, covered, for about 20 minutes. Check for doneness—stir it with a fork, and cook a bit longer if it is not done. When it is, set it aside. Heat a large skillet, melt the butter in it, and sauté the peppers and onion until almost finished. Add the mushrooms, cook them slightly, then add the rice and stir well.

Serves 6 to 8

Variation: Ann's Orzo Pilaf. Use orzo instead of rice, and do not cook it as long.

ORIENTAL HAWAIIAN FRUIT PILAF

- 3 ounces each dried figs, prunes, apricots, peaches, and dates
- 1/4 cup fresh dates
- 1/4 cup seedless raisins
- 1/4 cup each Madeira and plum wine
- 1 cup raw brown rice
- 1/2 teaspoon ground cinnamon
- 1/4 cup pine nuts
- Butter
- 1/4 cup chopped almonds

Soak the dried fruit in hot water for 1 hour. Drain, reserving the water. Marinate them, along with the fresh dates and raisins, in the wines for 30 minutes to 4 hours. Drain; measure the reserved soaking water and wine and add enough water to make 4 cups. Cook the rice in it. Keep in mind that it does take longer (up to 45 minutes) to cook brown rice than white rice. When the rice is done, stir in the cinammon and pine nuts. Put the rice in a buttered casserole, dot with butter, and bake in a preheated 350° oven for 10 minutes. Mix in the marinated fruit and garnish with the almonds.

Serves 6

Note: When you open a jar of pine nuts, refrigerate the unused part, as they quickly turn rancid.

POLYNESIAN GREEN RICE

- 3 tablespoons chopped scallions, green part only
- 2 1/2 tablespoons butter
- 1 1/2 tablespoons curry powder
- Salt
- 1 1/2 cups cooked rice
- 1/4 cup chopped fresh parsley
- 6 ounces chopped almonds
- 1 large pimiento, finely chopped
- 12 large spinach leaves
- 1/4 cup water
- 2 tablespoons rice wine

Sauté the scallions in the butter with the curry powder and just a dash of salt. Add to the rice, along with the parsley, almonds, and pimiento. Mix well. Put a large spoonful of this on each spinach leaf and roll up. Place the leaves in a large baking pan, add the water and wine, cover the pan, and bake in a preheated 400° oven for 30 minutes.

Serves 4

SPANISH RICE

- 1/2 pound bacon
- 1 cup raw rice
- 1/2 cup chopped onion
- 1/2 cup chopped green pepper
- 1 1-pound 4-ounce can tomatoes
- 1/4 cup chili sauce
- 1 teaspoon salt
- 1/2 teaspoon pepper

Chop the bacon into small pieces and cook in a large skillet. Remove the bacon, crumble it, and reserve. Leave the drippings in the skillet and sauté the rice, onion, and green pepper. Add the bacon and remaining ingredients, along with a tomato-can-ful of water, cover, and simmer for at least 45 minutes, until the rice is tender. Make sure everything is well mixed.

Serves 6

RICE STUFFING FOR TOMATOES, ZUCCHINI, OR EGGPLANT

- 1 cup raw rice
- 1/2 cup olive oil
- 1 medium onion, thinly sliced
- 1 large tomato, peeled and chopped
- 2 tablespoons pine nuts
- 2 tablespoons dried currants, soaked in water for at least 30 minutes and drained
- 1/2 tablespoon sugar
- Salt
- Pepper
- 2 tablespoons chopped fresh parsley
- 2 tablespoons chopped fresh dill
- 1/2 tablespoon thyme
- 6 tomatoes, zucchini, or eggplants, hollowed out

Wash the rice well and let it drain. In a very deep pan, heat the olive oil and fry the onion until soft. Add the chopped tomato, nuts, currants, sugar, salt, pepper, parsley, dill, and thyme. Stir in the rice and fry for 2 to 3 minutes. Add water to cover by 1/2 inch. Cover the pan and boil for 20 minutes, then only until the water is absorbed. Remove from the heat and let set for a few minutes. Uncover and let cool. Use the mixture to stuff the vegetables. Put them in a pan with a bit of water in the bottom. Bake, uncovered, at 350° for about 45 minutes, until they feel tender and done to your satisfaction.

Serves 6

RICE CROQUETTES

- 6 1/2 tablespoons butter
- 1/4 cup flour
- 2 1/4 cups milk, heated almost to a simmer
- 1 1/2 teaspoons salt
- 1/2 teaspoon nutmeg
- 1/8 teaspoon white pepper
- 3 cups cooked rice
- 5 egg yolks, beaten
- Wash: milk, cream, or beaten egg
- Cracker crumbs mixed with finely crushed nuts or very finely chopped dried raisins or prunes or fresh dates

Melt the butter in a saucepan, stir in the flour, and cook carefully, stirring, for a few minutes; do not let it brown. Add the milk gradually, stirring until it thickens and is smooth. Add the salt, nutmeg, pepper, and rice. Cook, stirring, until the mixture boils at the sides of the pan and leaves the bottom of the pan easily. A spoonful at a time, add 4 to 5 tablespoons of the hot rice mixture to the egg yolks, stirring constantly, then incorporate the egg yolks into the rice. Turn the mixture out onto a well-buttered flat pan, and cover with wax paper or greased paper to keep it from crusting. Let cool and refrigerate, to make it easier to handle. When it is cold, use an ice cream scoop for portions the size of an egg. Roll them into the desired shape, bread them, and fry in deep fat at 350° until golden brown.

Serves 6

VEGETABLE-RICE MEDLEY

- 3 cups chicken stock
- 1 large green pepper, seeded and dried
- 1 large red pepper, seeded and diced
- 1 large yellow onion, chopped
- 8 mushrooms, thinly sliced
- 8 florets each broccoli and cauliflower, each cut into 4 pieces
- 6 scallions, green part only, finely chopped
- 2 carrots, cut into small dice
- 2 cups cooked rice
- Pepper

Heat the chicken stock in a large pot and cook all of the vegetables. Drain, reserving the stock. Mix the rice with the cooked vegetables and season to taste. If the dish appears too dry, add just enough of the stock to make it slightly moist but not wet.

Serves 6

BAKED RICE AND CARROTS

- 6 slices bacon, diced
- 4 scallions, white part only, finely chopped
- 6 mushrooms, thinly sliced
- 1 1/2 cups finely diced carrots
- 3 cups cooked rice
- Salt
- Pepper
- 1 cup heavy cream
- 2 eggs, beaten

Cook the bacon, set aside, and sauté the scallions and then the mushrooms in the bacon drippings. Blanch the carrots in hot water for only a few minutes. Drain. Mix together all of the ingredients, except the cream and eggs. Put in a buttered large casserole. Whip the cream until fluffy and add the eggs. Fold into the rice mixture. Bake, covered, at 325° for at least 45 minutes. Remove the cover and, if need be, bake until the top is a light golden brown.

Serves 6

PORK FRIED RICE

- 8 ounces pork, finely chopped
- 1 onion, finely chopped
- 1/2 each green and red pepper, seeded and finely chopped
- 3 scallions, finely chopped
- 1 tablespoon light soy sauce
- 1 tablespoon dark soy sauce
- 1 tablespoon hoisin sauce
- Pepper
- 3 cups cooked rice
- 1/4 cup pork stock (optional)

In a heated skillet, cook the pork, then add the onion, green and red peppers, and scallions. Sauté for a few minutes; add the light and dark soy sauce and hoisin sauce. Season with pepper, add the rice, and heat through. If the mixture is too dry, add some pork stock. Toss all of this together and serve.

Serves 4

FRIED RICE, JAPANESE STYLE

- 2 tablespoons oil
- 6 small mushrooms
- 6 scallions, chopped
- 1 tablespoon dark soy sauce
- 2 tablespoons sake
- 1 1/2 cups cooked rice
- 2 eggs, beaten

Heat the skillet, heat the oil in it, add the mushrooms, scallions, soy sauce, and sake, and cook for a few minutes. Do not overcook it. Add the rice, stir well, and cook for 5 minutes or so. Add the eggs and cook, stirring, for a few minutes longer.

Serves 4

HOPPIN' JOHN

- 2 cups black-eyed peas
- 4 ounces somewhat lean bacon or salt pork, cut into small pieces
- 3 cups cooked rice
- 2 large pimientos, cut into medium dice
- Salt
- Pepper

Soak the peas overnight. Rinse them and put in a pot with about 1 quart water, along with the bacon or salt pork. Cook very slowly for at least 1 hour. Check for doneness. Add the rice and pimientos and season to taste.

Serves 6

Strictly southern style.

WILD RICE STUFFING

- Fat from a wild goose, duck, or other wild bird, even turkey
- 1/2 large onion, finely chopped
- 1 celery stalk, finely chopped
- 8 ounces pork sausage meat
- 1/2 Granny Smith apple, cored and chopped
- 1/2 cup cooked wild rice
- 1 cup cooked brown rice
- About 2 pinches of poultry seasoning

Render the fat from the bird and sauté the onion and celery in it. Drain off the fat. Break up the sausage and cook it in the pan with the onion and celery. When it is done, add the apple and cook until it is soft. Add the wild rice and brown rice, mix well, and season to taste.

Serves 4

Variation: Use bacon instead of sausage and add sautéed sliced mushrooms.

Wild rice (actually, not rice but a perennial grass native to North America) is harvested by hand by the Indians of Minnesota.

SALADS

There are as many variations as there are types of ingredients. You can add almost anything to a salad, or change it by varying the dressing (see pages 261–64.

It is true that romaine lettuce should be used for Caesar salad, but it is not gospel. If it is not available, use another. So what? There is Boston lettuce, iceberg, bibb, leaf, or even escarole. How about endive? Who says you can't use it? It's more expensive than the others, but you can still use it. A great many people like a more bitter type of green—kale, dandelion greens, spinach, or any other of the many mustard or sour grass types.

Learning to mix all sorts of vegetables with greens and dressings is the only thing you have to do. Use peppers—hot, mild, sweet, or even sour—tomatoes, eggs, radishes, celery, cabbages, and so on.

CHEF'S SALAD

1 head lettuce
8 ounces ham
2 green peppers, seeded and sliced into strips
4 mushrooms, thinly sliced
8 black olives
1 dill pickle, cut lengthwise into 4 slices
4 slices American cheese
4 slices Swiss cheese
1 pound turkey meat
4 hard-boiled eggs

Using lettuce as a base, mound the salad by arranging all of the ingredients decoratively. Top with a dressing of your choice.

Serves 4

CAESAR SALAD

1/2 cup salad oil
1 tablespoon Worcestershire sauce
3/4 teaspoon salt
1/2 teaspoon pepper
2 lemons
2 garlic cloves, cut in half
4 anchovies
1 large head romaine lettuce
1/2 cup crumbled blue cheese
1/4 cup freshly grated Parmesan cheese
1 egg
2 cups croutons

Combine the oil with the Worcestershire sauce, salt, pepper, and juice of 1/2 lemon. Set aside. Completely crush the garlic in the bottom of a large wooden bowl, rubbing it into the bowl with as much force as possible. Likewise, crush and rub in the anchovies. Break the romaine into nice bite-size pieces (do not cut it). Toss with the garlic and anchovies, sprinkle in the cheeses, pour in the dressing, and toss again. Break the egg over this. Drip on the juice of the remaining 1 1/2 lemons and then toss to mix well. Top with the croutons, toss once again, and serve.

Serves 4

SPINACH SALAD

- 1/4 cup Italian dressing (page 262, or use bottled dressing)
- 1/4 cup French dressing (page 262)
- 1/2 cup mayonnaise
- 1/2 tablespoon lemon juice
- 1 garlic clove, crushed
- Salt
- Pepper
- 2 bunches or 1 package spinach, washed and torn into pieces
- 2 eggs, hard-boiled, and chopped
- 4 slices bacon, cooked and crumbled
- 4 mushrooms, sliced

Combine the dressings, mayonnaise, lemon juice, garlic, salt, and pepper and mix well. Pour over the spinach and toss. Sprinkle the eggs, bacon, and mushrooms over each portion.

Serves 4

HOT SPINACH-FETA-RICOTTA CHEESE

- 1 1/2 pounds fresh spinach or 1 pound frozen spinach, thawed and well drained
- 4 tablespoons olive oil
- 2 garlic cloves, minced
- 1 large onion, chopped
- 2 jiggers dry vermouth
- Salt
- Pepper
- 10 ounces ricotta cheese
- 10 ounces feta cheese, crumbled
- 4 tablespoons chopped fresh parsley

If the spinach is fresh, wash it, break it up into small pieces, and sauté in oil with garlic and onion. When done, season with the vermouth, salt, and pepper. If the spinach is frozen, add the seasonings to it *before* sautéing.

Put the spinach in a large casserole dish. Mix the two cheeses with the parsley and place on top of the spinach. Bake in a preheated 360° oven until the cheese becomes golden brown.

Serves 4

CREOLE RICE SALAD

- 4 tablespoons olive oil
- 2 garlic cloves, minced
- 2 large pinches of Paul Prudhomme's Seafood Magic Seasoning
- 1/4 teaspoon Tabasco sauce
- 6 scallions, chopped
- 8 ounces chopped ham
- 12 ounces cooked shrimp, peeled, deveined, and cut into pieces
- 1 green pepper, seeded and chopped
- 3 cups cooked rice
- 3 tomatoes, chopped
- Leaf lettuce

In a blender, mix the oil, garlic, seafood seasoning, and Tabasco sauce. Place in a bowl and add the scallions, ham, shrimp, and green pepper. Mix well. Add the rice, mix, and chill until quite cool. Mix in the tomatoes and serve on a bed of lettuce.

Serves 4

Aspic and Gelatin Salads

A gelatin salad takes its flavor from the ingredients, rather than from the gelatin. Thus, you can make a gelatin salad by cutting up, say, fruit, cooking it in fruit juice and gelatin (softened in cold water), and pouring the mixture into a mold and chilling it. Roll the outside of the mold in hot water to loosen the salad, then turn it out onto a serving dish. Top it with a brandied cream sauce: whipped cream, sour cream, a bit of yogurt, and brandy (or bourbon), mixed to the desired consistency.

Aspic is made from a concentrated stock, which gels from the proteins extracted during cooking. If it is not firm enough —aspic from fish stock, for example—softened powdered gelatin can be added. Aspics can also be made from flavorful liquids such as tomato juice, as in the following recipe.

SHRIMP ASPIC SALAD

- 1 package unflavored gelatin
- 12 shrimp, peeled and deveined
- 1/2 large onion, cut into 1-inch dice
- 2 celery stalks, cut into 1-inch dice
- 1 pint tomato juice
- 4 tablespoons Chablis
- 1 teaspoon tarragon
- 1 tablespoon lemon juice

Prepare the gelatin according to the directions on the envelope. Heat all of the remaining ingredients together until the shrimp are cooked. Combine with the gelatin, pour into a mold, and refrigerate until firm. Dip the outside of the mold in hot water and invert onto a serving dish.

Serves 4

WILLIAM'S CHEESE SALAD

- 6 ounces cream cheese
- 1 cup light cream
- 1/4 cup ground almonds
- 1/4 cup chopped cashews
- 1/4 cup cold milk
- 2 tablespoons unflavored gelatin, softened in cold water
- 1 tablespoon tarragon vinegar
- 3/4 cup heavy cream
- 1 bunch watercress

Put the cream cheese and light cream in a double boiler and cook until completely blended, stirring often. Add the almonds and cashews. Combine the milk and gelatin. Add it to the cheese mixture and stir until completely incorporated. Let cool. Stir in the vinegar. Beat the heavy cream and fold it into the cheese mixture. Place in a mold, such as a ring mold, and chill. Unmold and serve on a bed of watercress, or with the watercress around the edges of the salad.

Serves 6

EGGS AND EGG DISHES

With all the cooking that is done with eggs, the general public knows so little about them that it is almost sinful. I will try to give you some of the pertinent facts concerning eggs.

Eggs are graded by weight, but the important thing is their freshness. They are further graded by flavor and appearance: grades AA to C—the best to the worst.

AA is an egg that is less than 24 hours old when it reaches the store, and and it is heavy; a dozen of these eggs weigh about 2 pounds. It is said that all grade AA and A eggs are okay for eating as is; grades B and C should be used only for baking. What is the distinction between B and C? I don't know—but I can tell you how to ascertain whether an egg is fresh or old.

Obviously, you cannot candle an egg at the store. Instead, hold it by your ear and shake it. A fresh egg just about fills the shell; as it grows older, the amount of albumen (white) shrinks. So if you hear very little sloshing, you know it is fairly fresh. If you hear a great deal of sloshing, put it back—it is too old.

Color does not have any bearing on the egg's nutritional value or its freshness. You may have heard that white eggs usually are stored for shipment and brown eggs are from local farmers only. Not true.

Eggshells are very porous, so odors can permeate the inside under poor storage conditions. Therefore, they should always be kept covered in your refrigerator.

Now that you have that down pat, let us get to cooking techniques. There are so many ways to cook eggs that people are often confused, but it's a simple thing to learn (as are most things in cooking).

Never cook eggs directly from the refrigerator. Allow them to reach room temperature, especially if you are going to cook them in the shell. Have you ever had them crack after you put them in the water? The cause is the shock of going from ice cold to boiling hot. At room temperature they will react well to any cooking technique.

Never boil eggs. To cook "hard-boiled" eggs, bring the water to a boil and then turn the heat down to a simmer.

Poaching eggs is not difficult, but you may have had trouble with the albumen spreading over the pan. Add a bit of vinegar to the water before putting in the egg. It will not affect the taste, but will keep the white from spreading.

Coddling eggs is done in special dishes, and the egg is cooked at just below the boiling point—nothing more, nothing less.

Shirred eggs are done in two ways. First, place an egg in a buttered shirred egg dish and cook it slowly on top of the stove until the white just begins to set, then transfer to a preheated 360° oven and finish cooking. Never overcook, for the purpose of shirring eggs is to serve them soft, not hard. The second way of preparing them is to butter the shirred dish, place the egg in it, and bake at 360° from start to finish.

There is no trick to making good scrambled eggs. Just follow this simple rule: not too hot, not too fast.

OMELETTE

3 eggs
1 ounce water
Butter

Sample Fillings

Jelly
Lox, cream cheese, and dill
Crab meat
Sautéed shrimp and garlic
Sautéed mushrooms and onions
Grated cheese
Assorted blanched vegetables

Beat the eggs and water thoroughly. Heat an omelette pan with a light coating of butter to high heat. Add the eggs and allow them to start to set. Stir slightly, pulling up the edges so liquid egg can run underneath. Add the filling. Place the pan under a broiler until the omelette fluffs. Fold the omelette and remove it to a plate.

Serves 1

Use room-temperature eggs to make the omelette fluffy. Make sure the omelette pan has a heatproof handle that can go under the broiler or in the oven.

FRENCH-STYLE OMELETTE

6 eggs
Salt
Pepper
1/2 cup milk
2 tablespoons butter
Filling (type and amount to taste)

Beat the eggs just enough to blend the whites and yolks. Stir in the salt, pepper, and milk. Melt the butter in a large skillet over low heat. When it just begins to bubble, pour in the egg mixture. Cook for a minute or so, until the edges start to firm up. Keep lifting the edges and letting the liquid pour under to continue cooking. When it is evenly cooked, add your filling—diced ham, pieces of cooked chicken, slices of cheese, or any type of jam or jelly. Fold it over, heat through, and serve.

Serves 2

CAVIAR OMELETTE

- 4 eggs, separated
- 3 tablespoons hot water
- 1/2 teaspoon salt
- Butter
- 1 tablespoon chopped chives
- 2 tablespoons caviar
- 2 tablespoons sour cream

Beat the egg yolks until light in color, then add the hot water and salt. Beat the egg whites until very stiff and fold them in. Butter an omelette pan well and heat it slightly. Pour in the omelette mixture and cook over a low flame until it sets (firms up). Put it under the broiler until golden but not too brown. Mix the chives, caviar, and sour cream into a loose but spreadable paste. Spread over the top of the omelette, fold it in half, and broil to a light golden color. Serve immediately. I like it with hollandaise sauce on top and potato pancakes.

Serves 2

A SPANISH OMELETTE OF CLASS

- 1 cup coarsely chopped onions
- 6 tablespoons butter
- 1/2 cup chopped cooked ham
- 1 cup canned tomatoes
- 1 tablespoon minced fresh parsley
- 1/2 teaspoon salt (optional)
- 1/2 cup white wine
- 1 cup cooked small shrimp
- 6 eggs, beaten

Sauté the onions in 4 tablespoons butter. Add the ham and tomatoes, parsley, salt, and wine. Set aside. Just before you are ready to add the mixture to the omelette, add the shrimp and heat through. Melt the remaining butter in a large skillet with a tight-fitting lid. Add the eggs, cover, and cook to let the bottom brown slightly. Turn and do the other side. Serve with the filling on top.

Serves 2

A GOURMET'S OMELETTE

- 1/3 cup plus 4 tablespoons butter
- 1/3 cup flour
- 1 1/2 cups milk
- 1/2 teaspoon salt
- Meat from 1 1-pound lobster
- 6 eggs, separated
- 2 tablespoons parsley sprigs

Melt the 1/3 cup butter in top of a double boiler; stir in the flour until it is smoothly blended. Add the milk and salt and place over boiling water. Cook, stirring constantly, until the mixture has thickened. Remove two thirds of the sauce and set aside to cool to room temperature. Add the lobster meat to the sauce in the double boiler and keep warm.

Beat the egg yolks until lightly colored and slightly thickened; add the cooled white sauce and heat to mix thoroughly. Beat the egg whites until stiff. Fold them into the egg yolk–cream mixture. Butter the inside of the lid of a 10-inch skillet and melt the remaining butter in the skillet. Pour in the egg mixture, smooth the top with a rubber spatula or a spoon, and cover the skillet. Cook over low heat for 15 minutes, or until the sides and the bottom of the omelette have turned a light golden brown and it has puffed up and cooked through.

Cut through the center with a sharp knife to within 1/2 inch of the bottom, loosen the omelette, and transfer it to a heated platter. Pour the lobster sauce over half the omelette and fold over the other half. Garnish with parsley.

Serves 2

APRICOT SOUFFLÉ OMELETTE

- 2 eggs, separated
- 1 tablespoon superfine sugar, plus extra for garnish
- 1 tablespoon butter
- 6 ounces hot cooked or canned apricot halves (3 to 4 whole apricots)

In a mixing bowl, with a wooden spoon beat the egg yolks, sugar, and 2 teaspoons water until creamy. Whisk the egg whites to the stiff-peaks stage. Gently fold them into the yolks.

Heat the butter in a 6- to 7-inch omelette pan until very hot. Add the eggs and cook until golden brown underneath. Put the pan under a hot grill and lightly brown the top of the omelette. Slide the omelette onto a heated serving plate and place the hot apricots on half of it. Fold over the other half and dust the top with the extra sugar.

Serves 1

SCRAMBLED EGGS, FRENCH STYLE

- 8 tablespoons (1 stick) butter
- 12 eggs, slightly beaten
- Salt
- Pepper
- About 1/2 cup heavy cream

Melt half of the butter in a very large skillet. Slowly add the eggs to the pan and, stirring with a wooden fork or spoon, cook over low heat until the eggs are firm but not hard. Remove the

pan from the heat. Put the remaining butter and the salt and pepper in the pan, and stir in just enough cream to make the dish rich. (If the eggs are very fresh, they will absorb most, if not all, of the suggested amounts of butter and cream.)
Serves 4

EGGS BENEDICT

- 8 slices (about 1 pound) Canadian bacon, sliced 1/8 inch thick
- 4 English muffins, split and toasted
- 8 poached eggs
- 1/2 pint hollandaise sauce (page 245)
- 8 black olives
- Parsley

Broil the bacon slightly, but do not dry it out with too much heat. Place a slice of bacon on each English muffin half. Top with a poached egg. Ladle 1 ounce of hollandaise sauce over each egg. Decorate the egg with a slice of black olive and garnish the plate with parsley.
Serves 4

BASIC SOUFFLÉ

- 3 eggs, separated, plus 3 egg whites
- 4 tablespoons melted butter
- 1 teaspoon plus sherry
- 1/4 cup sifted flour
- 1/3 cup milk
- Salt
- Pepper
- 1 cup grated cheddar or other cheese

In a mixing bowl large enough to hold all of the ingredients, whip the egg yolks with the melted butter, sherry, flour, milk, salt, and pepper. If it seems too thick, add a bit more milk.

In another bowl, whip the egg whites until they reach the soft-peaks stage; don't make them too stiff. Add the cheese and mix again, then fold into the egg yolk mixture. Pour into a 1 1/2- to 2-quart soufflé dish and set it in a pan of hot water. Bake on the middle shelf of a preheated 400° oven for at least 1 hour, until it has risen 1 1/2 to 2 inches over the top. Serve it as soon as possible, for it will fall; they always do.

Serves 4

Note: Caution! Never open the oven door during the cooking process. If you do, it will fall before you can serve it.

Variation: Chocolate and Brandy Soufflé. Substitute sweet chocolate for the cheese and use a good coffee brandy with it.

Soufflés are very easy to make. The basic ingredients are always egg whites, a liquid mixture of egg yolks and flavorings, butter, and flour. The liquid ingredients should always be about one third of the amount of the whites. You can add almost anything to the liquid mixture to make the soufflé of your choice, such as brandy or cognac, chocolate, cheese, or strawberries. Follow these simple rules and impress your friends.

BROCCOLI SOUFFLÉ

- 1/2 cup mayonnaise
- 1/4 cup sifted flour
- 1 1/2 cups milk
- 1 teaspoon salt
- Small amount of white pepper
- 6 tablespoons grated cheese
- 4 eggs, separated
- 1 10-ounce package frozen broccoli, thawed and drained

Combine the mayonnaise and flour and mix well. Heat it slowly, and slowly add the milk; stir constantly until thick. Add the salt, pepper, and cheese. Cook again for a short time. Let cool. Beat the egg yolks and stir them in, along with the broccoli. Beat the egg whites until stiff and fold them in. Pour into a buttered 1 1/2- to 2-quart soufflé dish and set it in a pan of hot water. Bake in a preheated 300° oven for 1 hour and 15 minutes.

Serves 4

Variations: Omit the salt and add 4 to 6 ounces chopped cooked ham. Replace the broccoli with any other vegetable you like.

SPINACH SOUFFLÉ

- 1 tablespoon grated Parmesan cheese
- 7 to 8 tablespoons butter
- 2 or 3 shallots, minced
- 1 10-ounce package frozen chopped spinach, thawed and drained
- 2 tablespoons lemon juice
- 5 tablespoons flour
- 1½ cups milk
- 1 teaspoon salt
- White pepper
- 6 eggs, separated, plus 1 egg white

Preheat the oven to 400°. Ordinarily you don't butter a soufflé dish, because it prevents the soufflé from rising up the sides of the dish, but for this soufflé butter a 2-quart soufflé dish and sprinkle the bottom and sides with the Parmesan cheese.

Melt 1 tablespoon butter in a heavy saucepan and sauté the shallots for 2 to 3 minutes. Add the spinach and lemon juice and cook over very low heat, stirring frequently, until all of the liquid has evaporated. This should take about 10 minutes. Set aside.

Melt the remaining butter in a heavy saucepan and, over low heat, stir in the flour with a wire whisk; remove from the heat. Bring the milk to a boil and add it to the butter-flour mixture. Whisk until very smooth. Add the salt and pepper and continue whisking until well blended. Let this white sauce cool a little. Beat the egg yolks into the sauce, one at a time. Stir in the spinach and set aside.

Beat the egg whites until they hold soft peaks. Stir some of this into the sauce, to make it easier to work in the remainder, then stir in the rest of the egg whites. Pour into the soufflé dish and set it in a pan of hot water. Put it in the oven and turn the heat down to 375°. Bake for 35 to 40 minutes, until the top is well puffed and nicely browned.

Serves 4

ASPARAGUS SOUFFLÉ

- 3 tablespoons melted butter
- 3 tablespoons flour
- 1 cup milk
- 1/3 cup heavy cream
- 4 eggs, separated
- 2 1/2 cups diced cooked asparagus
- 1/2 to 1 teaspoon salt

Blend the butter and flour, add the milk and cream gradually, and cook until thick, stirring constantly. Beat the egg yolks until lemon-colored and thick. Add the yolks, asparagus, and salt to the white sauce, mix, and remove from the heat. Beat the egg whites until very stiff and fold into the other ingredients. Pour into a buttered 1 1/2- to 2-quart soufflé dish and set it in a pan of hot water. Bake in a preheated 400° oven for about 20 minutes.

Serves 4

GRAND MARNIER SOUFFLÉ

- 2 tablespoons butter, softened
- 1/3 cup plus 3 tablespoons sugar
- 5 eggs, separated, plus 2 egg whites
- 1/4 cup Grand Marnier
- 1 tablespoon freshly grated orange zest
- 1/4 tablespoon cream of tartar

Grand Marnier Sauce

- 1 1/2 cups sugar
- 1/2 cup water
- Large pinch of cream of tartar
- 1 jigger Grand Marnier

Preheat the oven to 450°. Grease a 1 1/2- to 2-quart soufflé dish with the softened butter and sprinkle with the 3 tablespoons sugar. Discard any excess.

In a double boiler set over simmering water, beat the egg yolks until well blended. Slowly add the remaining sugar, and continue beating until the yolks are thick and pale yellow. Stir in the Grand Marnier and orange zest and set it over ice until quite cold, stirring occasionally with a wooden spoon.

Beat the egg whites and cream of tartar until stiff. Mix a few spoonfuls with the egg yolk mixture, then fold in the rest. Spoon into the soufflé dish to within 2 inches of the top. Smooth the top with a rubber spatula, then make a cap on the top by cutting a trench 1 inch deep 1 inch in from the edge of the dish. Set the dish in a pan of hot water and bake on the middle shelf of the oven for 2 minutes or so, then reduce the heat to 400°. Bake for another 25 to 30 minutes, until the soufflé has risen about 2 inches above the top of the dish.

Meanwhile, make the sauce. Cook 1 cup sugar with the water and cream of tartar. In a small saucepan, cook the remaining 1/2 cup sugar until it is caramelized. Add it to the mixture, along with the Grand Marnier. Serve hot with the soufflé.

Serves 4

Variation: Instead of the sauce, top the soufflé with powdered sugar.

CRÊPES

- 1/2 cup sifted flour
- 1 large egg
- 1 1/4 cups milk
- 1 tablespoon melted butter

Mix all of the ingredients in a food processor or blender. Let it relax for at least an hour before making the crêpes. The pancakes must be very thin, so use just enough butter in the skillet to prevent sticking. Pour in just enough batter to form a film, and cook gently on each side. Stack between sheets of wax paper, let cool, and refrigerate or freeze until ready to use.

To serve, melt a little butter in a pan and briefly heat the crêpes. Fill with anything you like—for a sweet crêpe, fruit; wine or liqueur; or sugar and citrus zest—and fold in quarters.

Makes 16

BAKING

Breads and Rolls

*B*aking is easy, but it is not simple. I will give two examples of how to make something neat and spiffy—the infamous dinner roll and the even more infamous French bread.

Breads and rolls can be brushed with various glazes before being baked. Each gives a different crust. Egg white mixed with water produces a dark, shiny crust. Plain water makes it softer and not quite as dark. Egg yolk makes it heavier and tastier. Milk results in a frosted glaze. Butter makes the top flaky and crackly.

GREAT DINNER ROLLS

- 2 packages dry yeast
- 1 cup lukewarm milk (100°)
- 1/4 teaspoon sugar
- 1/2 teaspoon salt
- 4 cups sifted white bread flour
- 1 egg, beaten

Dissolve the yeast in the warm milk. Add the sugar and salt and half of the flour. Beat in the egg with a wooden spoon. Add the rest of the flour and beat again. Cover with a damp kitchen towel and let it rise in the refrigerator overnight, or until doubled in bulk. Punch the dough down, and all you have to do after that is take small pieces of dough, shape them into small or medium-size rolls, and set them in a baking pan. Let them rise in a warm (75° to 80°), draft-free place (such as an unlighted oven) for 25 minutes. Brush the tops with egg yolk, milk, or melted butter to glaze them. Bake in a preheated 400° oven for 12 to 15 minutes, until golden brown.

Makes 18 to 24

Note: Test baked yeast goods for doneness with a toothpick, inserted in the thickest part. If it comes out clean, not wet or sticky, the baking is done. A good test for bread is to tap the loaf on the bottom; if it sounds hollow, it is done.

Try this recipe and really enjoy being able to serve fresh, hot dinner rolls anytime, with the dough ready and waiting in the refrigerator.

FRENCH BREAD

- Small pinch of sugar
- 1 1/4 cups warm water (110°)
- 1 1/2 packages dry yeast
- 4 cups sifted white bread flour
- 2 teaspoons salt

Stir the sugar into the warm water and sprinkle in the yeast. Let stand for 5 minutes or so, until the surface becomes frothy. Stir gently to mix in any dry particles. Sift the flour and salt into a large mixing bowl, pour in the yeast liquid, and mix to make a dough. Flour a board or counter and knead the dough on it for 5 to 10 minutes, until it becomes smooth and elastic. Sprinkle the dough with flour, to prevent it from forming a crust, cover with a damp kitchen towel, and let it rise at room temperature for 2 to 3 hours.

Knead the risen dough very quickly. Divide into 2 pieces and shape them into long rolls. Place them on floured baking sheet pans, cover the dough, and let stand in a warm, draft-free place for 30 minutes.

Slash the loaves diagonally several times with a sharp knife and brush with lukewarm water. Bake in a preheated 425° oven for 15 minutes, then reduce the heat to 350° and bake for 15 to 20 minutes, until the loaves are golden brown and crusty.

Makes 2 loaves

WHITE BREAD

- 9 to 10 cups sifted flour
- 1/4 cup sugar
- 1 teaspoon salt
- 2 envelopes dry yeast
- 1 quart heated milk (100°)
- 1 large egg

In an electric mixer, mix 3 cups flour with the sugar, salt, and yeast. Add the milk slowly and beat for 2 minutes at medium speed. Add the egg and 2 cups flour and beat for 2 minutes at high speed. Add the rest of the flour and knead for 8 to 10 minutes. Put in an oiled bowl, turn the dough to oil it on all sides, cover, and let rise in a warm, draft-free place until doubled in bulk. Punch down. Let rise again at 80° for 45 minutes. Bake in a preheated 400° oven for 15 to 20 minutes, until brown.

Makes 2 loaves

ANOTHER WHITE BREAD

1 cup warm water (110°)
Small pinch of ginger
2 tablespoons sugar
1 package dry yeast
2 teaspoons salt
2 tablespoons butter
1 cup milk, scalded and cooled
About 4 cups sifted flour (depending on the amount of moisture in the flour)
Olive oil

Mix the water, ginger, sugar, and yeast. Let sit until the yeast activates, 4 to 5 minutes. Add the salt, butter, and milk, stir, and start adding flour, about 2 cups in the beginning. Keep adding flour until it forms a sticky but cohesive dough. Add flour as required while kneading to get a satiny-smooth and soft dough. Roll it into a ball and lightly coat with olive oil. Cover it and let rise in a warm, draft-free place until doubled in bulk.

Punch it down and let rise again. Punch it down and let it sit for 10 minutes, then form into 2 loaves (or into rolls or buns or whatever). Again lightly coat with olive oil and let rise, set in pans or on sheets or whatever. Bake rolls or buns in a preheated 400° oven for 20 to 25 minutes. Bake bread at 400° for 15 minutes or more, until somewhat crusty and resistant, then turn the oven down to 375° and continue baking for 1 hour or more, until done. You can brush the tops with water, egg white, or butter during the baking, depending on the glaze you are looking to achieve.

Makes 2 loaves or 24 rolls or buns

SOURDOUGH STARTER

About 4 large potatoes
2 cups sifted flour
2 tablespoons sugar
1/2 teaspoon dry yeast

Boil the potatoes in their jackets until they fall to pieces. It may take even more than 4 potatoes, if they are old. Remove the potato skins and purée the potatoes and liquid. Let cool. Measure out the volume; if necessary, add water to make 2 cups. Add the remaining ingredients and beat until creamy.

Cover and set aside in a warm place to ferment. Use only after a week has gone by.

Keep the starter refrigerated. Replenish it as you use it up—use half or at most three quarters of it, cook up another batch, let it ferment, and replace the amount that you removed.

What to do with it? Try the following recipe.

Thanks to Mary, the owner of the Black Castle Lodge near Delta Junction, Alaska, I am in possession of one of the best sourdough starter recipes I have ever seen or used.

Don't even begin to think that all of the recipes in this book are mine, for they are not, and I am indebted to some great chefs and cooks from my past for such gifts.

FRENCH BREAD SOURDOUGH STYLE

- 1 cup sourdough starter
- 2 tablespoons sugar
- 1 1/2 cups warm water (110°)
- 6 cups flour
- 1 tablespoon salt
- 1/2 teaspoon baking soda

Mix the starter, sugar, water, and 3 cups flour in a large plastic bowl. Cover it with plastic wrap or a kitchen towel and let it stand at room temperature for at least 12 hours.

Combine the salt, soda, and 1 cup flour. Beat until it becomes smooth, adding enough of the remaining flour to make the dough soft. Turn it out onto a floured board and mix in enough of the remaining flour to make it stiff enough to knead. Knead for at least 10 minutes, then stretch and roll it into a French-style loaf. Put it on a greased cookie sheet, cover, and let rise in a warm, draft-free place for at least 2 hours, or until doubled in bulk. Slash the top of the loaf at an angle four or five times, then brush it with butter, milk, or water. Bake in a preheated 375° oven for 30 minutes, or until done.

Makes 1 loaf

POTATO RYE

- 2 tablespoons dry yeast
- 1 tablespoon sea salt
- 1 tablespoon caraway seeds
- 2 cups hot (but not boiling) potato water (reserved from having cooked the potatoes)
- 1 cup firmly packed hot mashed potatoes
- 4 cups whole-rye flour
- 2 to 2 1/2 cups whole-wheat flour
- Melted butter
- Cornmeal

In a large mixing bowl, combine the yeast, salt, caraway seeds, and potato water. Stir. Add the mashed potatoes and mix to distribute evenly. Stir in the rye flour, 2 cups at a time. Mix in 1 cup whole-wheat flour.

Spread 1 cup whole-wheat flour over a kneading board, scrape the batter onto the flour, and knead in the flour. Knead for 15 minutes after all of the flour is in; flour the board as required to handle the dough (up to 1/2 cup whole-wheat flour may be called for). If, after 15 minutes, you are not feeling resistance when you knead, knead for another 5 or 10 minutes. Form the dough into a ball and put it in an oiled mixing bowl. Turn the dough to oil it on all sides and let it rise, covered by a hot, wet kitchen towel, in a warm, draft-free place for 1 1/2 to 2 hours, until doubled in bulk.

Punch the dough down and knead out any large air bubbles. Cut the dough in half and knead each half into a smooth ball. Shape them into loaves about 8 × 4 inches. Brush a cookie sheet with melted butter and sprinkle with cornmeal. Set the loaves on the cookie sheet and, with a sharp or serrated knife, slash each loaf diagonally in three or four diagonal places, about 1/2 inch deep. Cover with a dry kitchen towel and let them rise again for 30 minutes to an hour.

Remove the towel and brush the loaves with water. Bake them in a preheated 375° oven for 15 minutes; brush again (or spray) with water and bake for another 35 minutes. Turn off the heat and let the loaves sit in the oven for 10 minutes. Rap the bottom crust for the hollow sound that indicates doneness. Let cool on a wire rack for half an hour.

Makes 2 loaves

Variation: Substituting all or part rye meal for the rye flour makes the bread chewier.

Rye breads call for a lot of kneading—at least 15 minutes. If you get tired partway, cover the dough with an inverted bowl and take a break.

SWEDISH RYE

- 2 tablespoons fennel seeds
- 2 tablespoons dry yeast
- 1/4 cup blackstrap molasses
- 1/4 cup honey
- 2 cups hot (but not boiling) potato water (from having cooked potatoes)
- 1 teaspoon sea salt
- Grated zest of 1 orange
- 1/4 cup vegetable oil
- 3 cups whole-rye flour
- 3 1/2 to 4 cups whole-wheat flour
- Melted butter
- Cornmeal
- Milk

With a mortar and pestle, or the back of a spoon against the mixing bowl, coarsely crush the fennel seeds. Add the yeast, molasses, honey, and potato water. Stir to mix. Add the salt, zest, and oil. Stir. Thoroughly mix in the rye flour, then 3 cups whole-wheat flour.

Spread 1/2 cup whole-wheat flour over the kneading board and scrape the batter onto the flour. Knead in. Knead for 15 minutes, using as much of the remaining 1/2 cup flour as necessary. Oil a mixing bowl, shape the dough into a ball, and turn it in the bowl to oil it on all sides. Cover with a hot, wet kitchen towel and set in a warm, draft-free place to rise for about 1 1/2 hours, until doubled in bulk.

Punch the dough down and knead it to eliminate large air

bubbles. Cut the dough into 3 pieces and roll them into 3 smooth balls. Roll each out into a loaf about 2 × 14 inches. Brush 2 cookie sheets with melted butter and sprinkle with a thin layer of cornmeal. Set the loaves on the sheets, prick the tops all over with a fork, cover with a dry towel, and let them rise again for 30 to 45 minutes.

With a light hand, brush the tops with milk, and bake in a preheated 375° oven for about 30 minutes. Rap the bottom to test for doneness and let cool on a wire rack for a few minutes. Serve hot.

Makes 3 loaves

Variations: Replace half or all of the potato water with beer, and increase the salt by 1 teaspoon.

For a hard crust, brush the bread twice with water (as for potato rye) instead of using milk.

Brushing the top with milk gives this bread a soft crust.

REFRIGERATOR RYE

- 2 tablespoons dry yeast
- 1 tablespoon sea salt
- 1/3 cup blackstrap molasses
- 1/4 cup vegetable oil
- 2 cups hot water
- 3 cups whole-rye flour
- 3 to 3 1/2 cups sifted white flour
- Melted butter

In a mixing bowl, combine the yeast, salt, molasses, oil, and hot water. Stir. Mix in the rye flour, then 2 cups white flour.

Spread 1 cup white flour over the kneading board and scrape the dough out onto it. Knead it, adding only as much of the remaining 1/2 cup white flour as necessary to keep the dough from sticking. When the dough stops sticking, knead for another 10 minutes. It will be cohesive and get quite springy as it approaches readiness. Divide it into 3 parts and shape each into a loaf to fit an 8 × 4 × 2-inch loaf pan. Brush the pans with melted butter and put a loaf in each. With your fingers, level the top of each loaf. Cover each pan with greased plastic wrap. Don't make the plastic taut and don't try to fasten it to the sides; it will rise with the dough. Set the pans in the refrigerator and let the loaves rise there for 5 to 24 hours.

Carefully remove the plastic wrap, and bake immediately in a preheated 375° oven for about 45 minutes. Test for doneness and let cool on a wire rack.

Makes 3 loaves

Variation: Add 1 tablespoon caraway, fennel, or anise seeds to the mixing bowl, or knead them in when shaping the loaves.

PUMPERNICKEL

- 3 tablespoons dry yeast
- 2 teaspoons sea salt
- 1/4 cup blackstrap molasses
- 1 tablespoon Postum or instant coffee powder
- 2 cups hot water
- 1/4 cup vegetable oil
- 2 cups whole-rye flour
- 2 cups whole-wheat flour
- 1 to 2 cups sifted white flour
- Melted butter
- White cornmeal

Glaze

- 1 teaspoon Postum or instant coffee dissolved in 2 teaspoons water

In a large mixing bowl, combine the yeast, salt, molasses, Postum, and hot water. Stir. Mix in the oil. Mix in the rye flour, then the whole-wheat flour.

Spread 1 cup white flour over the kneading board, scrape the batter out onto the board, and knead for 15 minutes, adding as much of the remaining white flour as necessary to keep the dough from sticking. Oil a mixing bowl, shape the dough into a ball, and turn it in the bowl to oil it on all sides. Cover with a hot, wet kitchen towel and set in a warm, draft-free place to rise, about 1 to 1 1/2 hours.

Punch the dough down, knead it briefly to eliminate large air bubbles, and cut it into 3 pieces. Shape them into round or oval loaves. Brush 2 large cookie sheets with melted butter and sprinkle with cornmeal. Set the loaves on the sheets, cover with a dry towel, and let them rise for 30 to 45 minutes.

Gently brush the tops with the glaze. Bake in a preheated 375° oven for 50 minutes to 1 hour. If the loaves look close to scorching after 50 minutes, but still seem raw, shut the oven off for the last 10 minutes of baking. Let cool on a wire rack and eat warm.

Makes 3 loaves

CROISSANTS

- 4 cups (1 pound) plus 5 tablespoons (or as needed) sifted flour, plus extra flour for dusting
- 5 tablespoons sugar
- 1 1/2 teaspoons salt
- 1 1/2 cups milk
- 1 1/2 packages dry yeast or 2/3 ounce fresh yeast
- 2 1/2 sticks (1 1/4 cups) unsalted butter, cold
- 1 egg, lightly beaten with 2 tablespoons milk

Combine the 4 cups flour, sugar, and salt in a large mixing bowl and stir with a wooden spoon to mix.

Heat the milk in a small heavy saucepan to about 100°, or mildly warm to the touch. Sprinkle dry yeast over the milk and let stand until the milk has soaked through all of the yeast particles (or crumble in the fresh yeast and let stand until dissolved). Whisk until thoroughly blended (feel the bottom and sides of the pan for lumps). Pour the mixture into the dry ingredients. With a wooden spoon, stir the dry mixture from the sides of the bowl into the center. When no dry flour or clumps of dampened flour can be seen, beat with the spoon for 30 seconds, until the dough is somewhat smoother but loose and sticky. Do not overwork it. Cover with plastic wrap and refrigerate for 8 hours or overnight. The dough will double in bulk and become very light and spongy.

The next day, sprinkle the 5 ounces of flour on a work surface. Cut the butter into thin slices lengthwise and press both sides in the flour; work quickly to keep the butter hard and cool. Press it all together to form a long loaf of butter with flour throughout. Refrigerate it for about an hour.

Remove the dough to the work surface. It will be too spongy and fragile to roll out, so use your hands to flatten it and stretch it out to about 8 × 14 inches. Lightly mark the dough into 3 sections. Take out the butter and break off small egg-size lumps. Press them flat, lay them over two thirds of the dough (keep a 1-inch border at the sides unbuttered), and fold the other section over it. Press the ends of the dough together to seal, using the palms of your hands, but don't flatten them too thin.

Dust the work surface with flour, lay the dough down on it gently, and gently work it with your hands to incorporate the butter throughout the layers of dough. With a rolling pin, gently press the dough down in ridges. Every so often, lift the dough to check that it does not stick to the work surface. Roll the dough out to about 10 × 24, then fold it into thirds, as in the previous paragraph. This completes the first turn. Always keeping the folded crease to your right, roll it out again to about 10 × 24 inches and about 1/4 inch thick. When you have done this twice (three turns in all), fold it again into thirds, wrap with plastic wrap, cover with a damp kitchen towel, and refrigerate for about 20 hours.

Flour the work surface and put the dough on it. Let it warm up for about 5 minutes. If necessary, you can gently warm it by pressing lightly with your palms; your body heat lets the buttered layers soften enough to be workable. Begin to work the dough, rolling it out with a rolling pin; be careful not to roll the very ends too thin. When it is about 9 × 18 inches, roll it out lengthwise and widthwise to about 10 × 24 inches. Fold it over into 3 layers and repeat (the dough has been turned a total of five times). Refrigerate the folded dough for about 2 hours; the total refrigeration time should come to no more than 24 hours.

To make croissants, flour the work surface and let it rest for about 5 minutes. Roll the dough out to about 18 × 21 inches and 1/4 inch thick. If you have a pastry wheel, use it to cut and trim the edges of the dough (reserve the trimmings) and also to cut the shape of the croissants, which is a triangle. Cut them evenly and put a piece of dough from the reserved trimmings in the centers, to make the croissants flakier. Roll them up, starting with the base of the triangle. Shape them into horseshoe forms, set on cookie sheets, and brush with the egg wash; do not let it drip on the cookie sheets. Let them rise until doubled in bulk, which could take from 45 minutes to 2 1/2 hours, depending on the warmth of the room.

Heat the oven to 375° and bake the croissants until a medium dark brown, about 25 minutes. The color should be uniform and there should be no white streaks along the creases.

Makes 18 to 20

Variations: Filled croissants. Mix diced ham and Dijon mustard, and perhaps some cheese. Fill the croissants, roll up, and bake. For a sweet filling, mix 1/3 cup blanched almonds, 1/2 cup sugar, 1/4 teaspoon cinnamon, and 1 egg white. Put about 1 tablespoon in each croissant, roll up, let rise, and bake.

Chocolate-Filled Croissants. Chop up semisweet chocolate into pieces the size of small peas. Cut the croissant dough into squares and put pieces of chocolate in each, just a bit off center. Brush the edges with egg wash, fold it in thirds, brush the top with melted butter, and bake.

MY FAVORITE CROISSANT

3 3/4 cups sifted flour
2/3 to 1 ounce dry yeast
1 cup lukewarm milk (100°)
Pinch of salt
1 1/2 sticks (3/4 cup) butter, softened

Sift the flour onto a board, make a well in the center, put the yeast in the well, and moisten it with a bit of milk. Mix in one quarter of the flour and let rise. Add the salt, butter, and remaining milk, and mix in all of the flour, moistening with additional milk if necessary. The dough should be firm, though, rather than soft. Roll it into a ball, cover with a damp cloth, and let rise in a warm, draft-free place.

Divide the dough into pieces about the size of an egg. Roll them out into ovals with a floured rolling pin. (If you prefer, roll out the dough in large sheets and cut them into triangles.) Roll up each piece and curve it into a crescent. Place them on a cookie sheet, let them rise, and brush with a little extra milk. Bake in a hot preheated 375° oven for 8 to 12 minutes, until golden brown. When you remove them from the oven, brush them very lightly with melted butter.

Makes 18 to 20

PIZZA

- 1/2 envelope dry yeast
- 1/3 cup warm water (110°)
- 1 1/2 cups sifted flour
- 2 teaspoons salt
- 4 tablespoons butter
- 1 egg, beaten

Suggested Toppings

- Spaghetti sauce (page 126)
- 1 pound mozzarella cheese, sliced
- 1 pepperoni, sliced
- 4 to 5 mushrooms, sliced and sautéed
- Oregano
- 1 green pepper, seeded and sliced
- Black olives, sliced
- Pepper

Soften the yeast in the water. Sift the flour and 1 teaspoon salt into a bowl. Work in the butter with your fingers. Add the egg to the yeast, then stir into the flour mixture until a ball of dough is formed. If it is too stiff, add a little more water. Knead on a lightly floured surface until smooth and elastic. Form into a ball, place in an oiled bowl, turn to oil the dough on all sides, cover with a towel, and let rise in a warm place for 2 hours. Divide the dough in half and roll out for 2 8-inch pizzas.

Spread spaghetti sauce on the dough and top with whatever

you like, in amounts to your taste. Bake in a preheated 400° oven for 10 to 12 minutes, watching that it doesn't burn on top.

Makes 2 8-inch pizzas

STICKY BUNS

- 1 package dry yeast
- 1/2 cup warm water (110°)
- 1/2 cup plus 1 pinch sugar
- 1 cup milk
- 8 tablespoons melted butter (1 stick)
- 3 1/2 cups sifted flour
- 1/4 teaspoon salt
- 2 egg yolks
- 1 teaspoon grated lemon zest
- 1 teaspoon cinnamon
- 1/2 cup currants or raisins
- 1 1/2 cups firmly packed brown sugar
- 4 tablespoons butter
- 1/2 cup coarsely chopped walnuts

Sprinkle the yeast into the warm water, along with the pinch of sugar. Let stand for 2 to 3 minutes, then stir to dissolve the yeast. Set in warm, draft-free place for 5 to 8 minutes, or until it has begun to bubble and is almost doubled in volume.

Pour the milk into a heavy 1-quart saucepan and warm it over medium heat until bubbles form around the edges of the pan. Turn the heat to low and add 4 tablespoons melted butter and 1/4 cup of the sugar. Stir until the sugar dissolves, then let cool to lukewarm and add the yeast mixture.

Sift the flour and salt into a deep mixing bowl. Make a well and pour into it the yeast mixture, egg yolks, and lemon zest. With your hands or a wooden spoon, work the flour into the other ingredients until it forms a medium-firm dough. On a lightly floured surface, knead the dough by folding it end to end, then pressing it down and pushing forward several times with the heel of your hand. Sprinkle the dough with a little extra flour whenever necessary to keep it from sticking to the board. Knead until the dough becomes smooth and elastic, about 10 minutes. Shape the dough into a ball and put it in a buttered large bowl. Dust the top with just a bit of flour, cover with a kitchen towel, and set in a warm place. It should double in about an hour.

Punch the dough down, then knead it briefly on a lightly floured board. Roll it out into a rectangle 12 inches long and 1/4 inch thick. Brush with 3 tablespoons melted butter. Combine the remaining 1/4 cup sugar with the cinnamon and currants, and sprinkle evenly over the dough.

In a small heavy saucepan, combine the brown sugar and 4 tablespoons butter with 1/2 cup water. Stir until the sugar dissolves; bring to a boil over high heat. Reduce the heat to moderate and cook the syrup for about 10 minutes, until it has the consistency and color of maple syrup. Let the syrup cool slightly, then drizzle half of it over the dough. Roll the dough into a tight cylinder about 2 inches in diameter, and cut it crosswise into 1-inch rounds.

Grease a 10-inch round cake pan with the remaining 1 teaspoon melted butter, pour in the remaining syrup, and sprinkle evenly with the chopped nuts. Arrange the rounds, on their side, in a circle around the edge of the pan; continue the pattern with the remaining rounds until the pan is full. Let them rise in a warm, draft-free place for about 25 minutes, until doubled in bulk. Heat the oven to 350° and bake the buns in the middle of the oven for about 30 minutes. When the buns are golden brown and firm to the touch, remove them from the oven and invert onto a cake rack. Separate and serve.

Makes 1 dozen

MUFFINS

- 2 cups sifted flour
- 3 teaspoons baking powder
- 1/2 teaspoon salt
- 1/4 cup sugar
- 1/4 cup butter or margarine, softened
- 1 cup milk
- 1 egg

Sift all of the dry ingredients into a mixing bowl. Mix well. Add the butter, milk, and egg. Mix just to blend; do not overmix. Butter a muffin tin, fill the cups about two thirds full, and bake in a preheated 400° oven for 25 to 30 minutes.

Makes 1 dozen

Variations: Whole Wheat Muffins. Substitute 1 cup whole wheat flour for 1 of the cups all-purpose flour and reduce the baking powder from 3 teaspoons to 2.

Sour Milk Muffins. Substitute 1 cup sour milk for regular milk and use only 2 teaspoons baking powder plus 1/2 teaspoon baking soda.

Most people love muffins, but few realize how simple they are to make.

SWEET MUFFINS

- 1 1/2 cups sifted flour
- 2 teaspoons baking powder
- 1/4 cup shortening or butter, softened
- 1/2 cup milk
- 1/2 cup sugar
- 1/2 teaspoon salt
- 1 egg

Prepare as in the previous recipe.

Makes 1 dozen

Variations: Apple Muffins. Add 1 teaspoon cinnamon and 1 cup chopped apple with the liquid ingredients. Bake for 30 minutes, or until done.

Blueberry Muffins. Add 1 cup fresh blueberries or 3/4 cup drained canned or thawed frozen blueberries.

BAKING POWDER BISCUITS

- 2 cups sifted flour
- 1 teaspoon sugar
- 3 teaspoons baking powder
- 1/2 teaspoon salt
- 4 tablespoons butter or shortening
- 3/4 cup milk

Sift the dry ingredients into a bowl, then work in the butter until it is evenly mixed and crumbly. Add the milk all at once, stirring only until the dough is puffy soft. Scoop out the dough onto a lightly floured pastry cloth. Flour your hands, pat the dough into a thick square, then squeeze it together. Knead 5 or 6 times so the biscuits will rise evenly. Pat out the dough to a square 1 inch thick. Dip a 2-inch cutter in flour and cut out the biscuits, working from the outside in, so there will be very few scraps to reroll. Set the rounds 1 inch apart on a greased cookie sheet and bake in a preheated 425° oven for about 12 minutes, until golden brown.

Makes 10 to 12

POPOVERS

- 1 cup sifted flour
- 2 eggs
- 1 cup milk
- 1/2 teaspoon salt

Heat the oven to 425°. In an electric mixer, beat all of the ingredients until very smooth. Butter large muffin tins or large timbale cups and put them in the oven until smoking hot. Fill them three quarters full of batter. Bake for 35 to 40 minutes, until crisp and golden brown. Don't open the oven door to look at them. If you have a glass door, fine; if not, wait the prescribed time before opening the door.

Makes about 8

SESAME WAFERS

- 8 tablespoons (1 stick) butter, softened
- 1 1/2 cups light brown sugar
- 1 egg
- 4 cups flour
- 2 large pinches baking powder
- 1 teaspoon vanilla extract
- 1 cup toasted sesame seeds

In a mixing bowl, cream the butter, sugar, and egg. Mix the flour and baking powder and stir in. Beat well. Add the vanilla extract and sesame seeds and beat to mix well. Put about 1 teaspoon per wafer on greased cookie sheets and bake in a preheated 350° oven for 9 to 10 minutes. Let cool somewhat on the cookie sheets, then set them on racks to finish cooling.

Makes 9 dozen

Pastry

PUFF PASTRY

5	cups sifted flour	$2^1/_4$	cups cold water
11	sticks ($5^1/_2$ cups, $2^3/_4$ pounds) butter	$^1/_2$	teaspoon salt
		3	small or 2 large eggs

In an electric mixer, mix the flour, 1 stick butter, water, salt, and egg. Take the dough out of the mixer and roll it into a ball, then let the dough stand for about 20 minutes.

Lay the dough on a floured work surface and roll it out to a 14- to 16-inch square, leaving the center of the dough a bit thicker than the edges. Put the remaining 10 sticks butter in the center of the dough. Fold the corners of the square into the center, overlapping one another. Flatten out with a rolling pin, then roll out to form a rectangle about $^1/_2$ inch thick. Brush off any excess flour and fold the dough into thirds, as you would fold a business letter to fit into an envelope, first one side over, then the other. Refrigerate for half an hour.

Take it out, roll it out and fold it again, and put it back in the refrigerator. Repeat this procedure at least four times.

After the last chilling, cut it to the size you need. Bake in a preheated 375° oven for 25 to 30 minutes, until it is nice and crisp.

Makes about 50 squares

Note: The dough can be kept refrigerated or frozen, but you must always roll it out again and let it come to room temperature (about half an hour) before cutting and baking it.

Puff Pastry Desserts: Napoleons. Roll out the puff pastry very thin and bake on a cookie sheet. Take it out and cut the pastry into 3 pieces. Spread the first piece with a soft custard (page 223), top with another layer, fill again, top again, and then top this with a vanilla frosting. Streak with lines of melted chocolate, and draw a knife across the frosting to make the characteristic design.

Cream Slices. Make napoleons and fill with a flavored whipped cream or Bavarian cream (page 224).

Nut Pastry. Roll out the dough, butter it slightly, sprinkle crushed almonds, pecans, or walnuts on it. Cut into pieces about 2 × 4 inches and bake as above. Take them out, cut in half, and fill with anything you like.

Apple Turnovers. Brush pastry dough squares with water, fill with apples (cooked with sugar, lemon juice, and cinnamon) in the center, fold into a triangle, brush with water or egg wash, and bake.

With this pastry dough you can make so many different desserts that you will never be at a loss as to what to serve guests. You must follow the formula exactly for it to come out right. (Or see the next recipe.)

EASY PUFF PASTRY

- 1/2 cup water
- 4 tablespoons butter
- 1/2 cup sifted flour
- 1/4 teaspoon salt
- 2 eggs

Put the water in a pan, bring to a boil, and add the butter; cook, stirring until melted. Mix together the flour and salt and stir it in with a wooden spoon over low heat. When it begins to pull away from the pan it is ready. Remove it from the heat and add the eggs, one at a time, beating vigorously after each addition. Put the mixture in a pastry tube and pipe it onto a greased cookie sheet. Bake in a preheated 450° oven for 5 minutes, then at 375° for 40 minutes. *Never open the oven door while baking this type of pastry.*

Makes 6 tart shells or 2 pie crusts

ÉCLAIRS OR CREAM PUFFS

Pâte à Choux

1 cup water
4 tablespoons butter
1 cup sifted all-purpose or bread flour
Pinch of salt
4 eggs, beaten

Filling

2 cups heavy cream
1/2 cup sugar
1 teaspoon instant coffee

Heat the water and butter to a boil. Add the flour and salt all at once. Stirring with a wooden spoon, cook over low heat until the mixture becomes very smooth and rolls away from the sides of the pan. Take it off the heat, transfer to a large bowl, and let cool slightly. Add the eggs, one at a time, beating well after each addition. Use to fill a pastry bag with a fluted nozzle and squeeze out hot-dog shapes, éclairs, or round shapes, for cream puffs. Bake on a buttered cookie sheet in a preheated 400° oven for 30 minutes. *Do not open the oven at any time during the baking.*

Whip the cream to the soft-peaks stage, then begin whipping in the sugar and coffee powder. Pipe into the cooled pastry—from the end for éclairs, from the side for cream puffs.

Makes about 1 dozen

Variation: Instead of instant coffee, use coffee extract or vanilla extract.

PIE CRUST

2 cups (1 pound) sifted pastry flour
1/4 teaspoon salt
1 1/4 cups lard or shortening
6 ounces plus ice water

Mix the flour and salt in a mixing bowl, add the lard, and rub together to the size of walnuts, for a flaky crust, or small peas, for mealy crust. Begin adding the ice water. Mix the dough with your hands until it just comes together, but *do not overwork it.* Once it has reached a form of dough, stop; just roll it together, put it on a floured board, and roll it out gently. The less you handle it the flakier it will be.

You can use this crust for any type of pie. You can top any pie with the same crust, or make an open type. If you make an open pie, first partially bake the crust in a preheated 400° oven for 8 to 12 minutes, weighted with dried beans or marbles. This cooking ensures that the crust will not be too mealy on the bottom. The total baking time for exposed pie crust should come to no more than 24 to 30 minutes. If a filling recipe calls for more time than that, wrap the exposed crust with foil to keep it from burning.

Makes 1 double-crust pie or 2 bottom-crust pies

Variation: Quick Sweet Pastry Dough. Use butter rather than lard or shortening, mix with the flour and salt, plus 1/4 cup sugar, and add a package of dry yeast dissolved in a bit of lukewarm water; let it set for a few minutes before adding the ice water. Roll out and cut into the desired shape.

FLAN PASTRY

2 1/2 cups sifted flour
Small pinch of salt
14 tablespoons (7 ounces) butter
1/3 cup sugar
1 egg

Sift the flour and salt into a mixing bowl and, using a fork or knife, mix in the butter evenly. Mix in the sugar and egg and make into a dough. Wrap it up and refrigerate for at least 1 to 3 hours. When you are ready to use it, roll it out, place it in an 11- to 12-inch flan pan, and bake as for pie crust, weighted with dried beans or marbles. Fill it with a custard. Depending on the filling, make a lattice topping or, as is more usual, leave the top open.

Makes 1 11- to 12-inch flan

Variations: You can make any type of fruit flan by proceeding as for a fruit pie; or just make a bottom glaze for the baked pastry, place cooked fruit on it, and top with another glaze or a cooked mixed fruit topping. For example, put a coating of cream cheese on the pastry and place fresh blueberries or strawberries on it; cook 1 to 2 cups berries with sugar and a bit of brandy, thicken with a bit of arrowroot powder mixed with a bit of water, and pour over the fresh berries. Bake in a preheated 375° oven for 35 to 40 minutes. Take it out and let cool on a rack. Top with powdered sugar or whipped cream.

APPLE STRUDEL

Pastry

- 1/2 cup warm water
- 2 tablespoons plus vegetable oil
- 1 tablespoon sugar
- 2 cups sifted flour
- 1 egg plus 1 egg white

- 8 tart green apples
- 2 tablespoons lemon juice
- Melted butter
- 1/4 cup granulated sugar
- 1/4 cup firmly packed light brown sugar
- Freshly grated cinnamon, nutmeg, and lemon zest
- 1/2 cup ground toasted almonds
- Powdered sugar
- Whipped cream (optional)

Make the pastry by blending the water, 2 tablespoons oil, and sugar in a small bowl. Mound the flour on a work surface, make a well in the center, and put the liquid mixture, egg, and egg white in the well. Gradually draw flour from the inner edge of the well into the center until all of the flour is incorporated. Gather the dough into a ball and slap it on the counter 100 times to develop the gluten. Rub the dough with oil, cover with an inverted bowl, and let stand for 30 minutes.

For the filling, peel, core, and thinly slice the apples. Sprinkle with lemon juice.

To assemble, oil a baking sheet pan and lightly oil your hands. Set the dough on a 48-inch round table covered with a tablecloth. Flatten the dough into a disk and press it into a large circle. Begin stretching the dough, pushing and pulling from the center outward, until it covers the entire table; it will be completely translucent. (Use floured cups to weight the edges.) Cut off and discard the thick edge of dough hanging over the table.

Heat the oven to 425°. Brush the dough with melted butter. Arrange the apple slices over three fourths of the dough and then sprinkle them with the sugars and dust with cinnamon, nutmeg, and lemon zest. Sprinkle the almonds over all of the dough. Using the tablecloth as an aid, roll the dough up into a log; tuck in the ends.

Set the strudel in the pan, formed into a U. Brush with melted butter. Bake for 15 minutes and brush again with butter. Reduce the oven temperature to 350° and bake for about 30 minutes, until golden brown. Let cool slightly in the pan. Cut into 2-inch pieces and sprinkle lightly with powdered sugar. Serve with either more powdered sugar over them or with whipped cream.

Serves 16

Cakes, Pies, and Tarts

CHOCOLATE MOUSSE CAKE

7 ounces semisweet chocolate
8 tablespoons (1 stick) unsalted butter
7 eggs, separated, at room temperature
1 cup sugar
1 teaspoon vanilla extract
1/8 teaspoon lemon juice

Heat the oven to 325°. Melt the chocolate and butter in a double boiler over simmering water. Stir until smooth. Whisk the yolks and 3/4 cup sugar until pale yellow and fluffy. Gradually stir in the chocolate and vanilla extract. Beat the whites with lemon juice until soft peaks form. Add the remaining sugar, 1 tablespoon at a time, and continue beating until stiff but not dry. Gently fold into the chocolate mixture. Pour three fourths of the batter into a buttered 9-inch springform pan; cover and refrigerate the remaining batter. Bake the cake for 35 minutes. Let cool completely. (The cake will fall as it cools, but don't let it bother you.) Trim the edges with a sharp knife and spread the remaining batter over the top. Refrigerate for at least 8 hours.

Makes 1 9-inch cake

BOURBON CHOCOLATE PECAN CAKE

12 ounces semisweet chocolate
2 sticks (1 cup) butter
8 eggs, separated
3/4 cup sugar
1/2 cup bourbon
1 pound ground pecans

Glaze

- 1 pound semisweet chocolate, melted
- 1/3 cup vegetable oil
- Pecan halves

*I*n a double boiler over simmering water, mix and melt the chocolate and butter. Beat the egg yolks and sugar, and mix in the chocolate, a little at a time. Add the bourbon and mix. Beat the egg whites until stiff and fold them in, along with the pecans. Butter and sugar the bottom and sides of a 9-inch springform pan and, if you have some on hand, put baking paper on the bottom. Pour in the batter and bake in a preheated 300° oven for 1 1/2 to 1 3/4 hours. Let cool.

Mix the glaze, pour over the cake, and let set until firm. Garnish with pecan halves.

Makes 1 9-inch cake

LOUISIANA PECAN CAKE

- 1 1/2 packages seedless raisins, cut into halves
- 1 cup whiskey
- 2 sticks (1 cup) butter, softened
- 2 1/2 cups granulated sugar
- 1 nutmeg, grated
- 6 eggs, beaten
- 4 1/2 cups sifted flour
- 3 1/2 cups coarsely chopped pecans
- 2 teaspoons baking powder
- 1 teaspoon salt
- Confectioner's sugar

*S*oak the raisins in whiskey overnight; drain (you can drink the whiskey, which has fulfilled its purpose here). Cream the butter and granulated sugar. Add the nutmeg and eggs and beat thoroughly. Mix 1 cup of the flour with the nuts. Sift together the remaining flour, baking powder, and salt. Add the dry ingredients to the creamed mixture. Fold in the nuts, then the raisins. Mix lightly and pour into a well-buttered and well-floured 10-inch tube pan. Bake in a preheated 350° oven for 1 hour and 25 minutes, or until the cake tests done. Do not overbake. Let cool in the pan for 5 minutes, turn it out, and let cool on a cake rack. Sprinkle with confectioner's sugar.

Serves 6 to 8

FRUIT CAKE ROLL

- 2 tablespoons butter, softened
- 1/2 cup sifted flour, plus extra as needed
- 4 eggs, separated
- Pinch of salt
- 1/4 cup sugar
- 1/2 teaspoon vanilla extract

Filling

- 1 1/2 cups heavy cream, chilled
- 4 tablespoons granulated sugar
- 1 12-ounce can crushed pineapple, thoroughly drained
- 1 to 2 teaspoons orange juice, or 1 cup marmalade or apricot preserves

- 3 tablespoons confectioner's sugar (optional)

Butter the bottom and sides of a 16 × 11-inch jelly roll pan. Line the pan with a strip of wax paper; let the extra paper extend over the edges. Use the remaining butter on the wax paper, and scatter a small handful of flour over it. Shake off the excess flour.

Heat the oven to 400°. In a mixing bowl, beat the egg whites and salt until they form soft peaks. Add the sugar, 2 tablespoons at a time, and beat until the whites cling solidly to the lifted beater. In another small bowl, beat egg yolks for about a minute, then add the vanilla extract. Mix in a large tablespoonful of the whites, then pour it over the egg whites. Fold together, adding the 1/2 cup flour, 2 tablespoons at a time.

Pour the batter into the jelly roll pan and spread it out evenly. Bake for about 12 minutes, until the cake draws slightly away from the sides of the pan, and a small knife inserted in the center comes out dry and clean. Turn it out on a double thickness of wax paper about 22 inches long. Remove the wax paper lining from the top of the cake and let cool to room temperature.

Beat the cream until slightly thickened, then pour in the granulated sugar and continue to beat to the stiff-peaks stage. With a rubber spatula, fold it into the pineapple and juice or marmalade. Spread the mixture evenly over the cake. Roll it up as you would a jelly roll and serve as is or chilled. If you used the orange juice, shake confectioner's sugar over the roll.

Serves 8

FRESH PEACH COBBLER

- 1 1/2 cups sugar
- 2 tablespoons cornstarch
- 2 cups boiling water
- 6 cups sliced peeled peaches
- 3 teaspoons butter
- 1 teaspoon cinnamon

Shortcake

- 6 tablespoons shortening
- 2 cups sifted flour
- 2/3 cup milk
- 3 teaspoons baking powder
- 2 tablespoons sugar

Mix the sugar and cornstarch and stir in the boiling water. Bring to a boil and continue boiling for 1 minute. Add the fruit. Pour into a baking dish, dot with butter, and sprinkle with cinnamon.

Sift together the dry ingredients and rub in the shortening with your hands until little beads form. Stir in the milk. Roll out on a floured board until 1/2 inch thick. Cut into desired shapes with a cookie cutter.

Top the fruit with the shortcake dough. Bake in a preheated 400° oven for 30 minutes.

Serves 12

FRESH COCONUT CREAM PIE

- 1 cup sugar
- 1/2 cup cornstarch
- 1/4 teaspoon salt
- 3 cups hot milk
- 3 egg yolks, beaten
- 1 teaspoon vanilla extract
- 1/2 teaspoon almond extract
- 2 cups grated fresh coconut, or 2 31/2-ounce cans flaked coconut plus 1/2 cup sugar
- 1 baked 9-inch pie shell (page 185)
- 1 cup heavy cream

Combine the sugar, cornstarch, and salt in a saucepan. Add the milk and bring to a boil over medium heat, stirring constantly. Boil for 2 minutes and take off the heat. Stir half of the hot mixture into the egg yolks, then combine with the rest of it. Cook, stirring, over low heat until it boils and is thick enough to mound from the spoon, about 5 minutes. Turn into a bowl and stir in the extracts and half of the coconut. Place wax paper directly on the filling and refrigerate for 1 hour. Turn into the pie shell and refrigerate for 3 hours. Whip the cream and spread it over the pie. Top with the remaining coconut.

Makes 1 9-inch pie

CRANBERRY CREAM PIE

- 1 12-ounce package fresh cranberries
- 11/4 cups sugar
- 1 cup water
- 2 egg yolks, at room temperature
- 2 tablespoons cornstarch
- 1 cup sour cream, at room temperature
- 1 baked 9-inch pie shell (page 185)
- Whipped cream

Combine the cranberries, 1 cup sugar, and the water in a heavy saucepan. Cook over medium-high heat until very thick, about 10 minutes. Mix the yolks, remaining sugar, and cornstarch. Add to the cranberries, stir in the sour cream, and cook until thick, about 4 minutes. Spoon into the shell and refrigerate for at least 8 hours or overnight. Spoon on whipped cream and serve.

Makes 1 9-inch pie

PECAN TARTS

- 4 eggs, beaten
- 1 1/2 cups dark brown corn sugar
- 1 1/2 tablespoons melted butter
- 1 1/2 teaspoons vanilla extract
- 1/4 teaspoon salt
- 1 1/4 cups chopped pecans
- Unbaked pastry for 14 to 18 tart shells (page 185)

Beat the eggs, sugar, melted butter, vanilla extract, and salt. Add the nuts and mix lightly. Pour into pastry-lined tart pans and bake in a preheated 400° oven for 10 minutes. Reduce the heat to 300° and bake for 20 to 30 minutes, until the filling is set.

Makes 14 to 18

HONEY NUT TART

Dough

- 1/2 cup sugar
- 2 sticks (1 cup) butter
- 1 egg plus 1 egg yolk
- 2 1/2 cups sifted flour
- Pinch of salt

Filling

- 2/3 cup sugar
- 3 tablespoons butter
- 2 tablespoons water
- 1/2 cup heavy cream
- 2 tablespoons honey
- 3 cups mixed nuts (walnuts, pecans, sliced almonds)

In an electric mixer at low speed, combine the sugar and butter. Add the egg and yolk, then the flour and salt. Knead into a ball and refrigerate for 1 hour. On a floured surface, roll out the dough to fit a 9-inch tart pan. Bake the shell in a preheated 375° oven for 10 minutes.

For the filling, cook the sugar with butter and water until dissolved. Continue cooking until the mixture caramelizes and turns a golden tan. Remove from the heat and stir; gradually add the cream. Add the honey and cook for 1 minute, making sure the lumps are out. Add the nuts and coat them well with the caramel. Pour into the tart shell and bake in a preheated 350° oven for 20 to 25 minutes. Let cool completely before serving.

Makes 1 9-inch tart

From Jo Anne Gretta, pastry chef instructor: "A favorite German recipe I found in Santa Barbara, California."

Cheesecake

*A*s these recipes show, there is much to be said about cheesecake, and there are many ways to make it.

RICH CREAM CHEESE CAKE

Shortbread

- 1 3/4 cups sifted flour
- 1 stick (8 tablespoons) butter, cut into small pieces
- 5 tablespoons sugar
- 1 egg yolk
- Pinch of salt
- Grated zest of 1 lemon

Filling

- 1 cup milk
- 3/4 cup plus 2 tablespoons granulated sugar
- Pinch of salt
- Grated zest of 1 lemon
- 4 egg yolks
- 2 envelopes unflavored gelatin, softened in cold water
- 2 cups heavy cream
- 1 pound cream cheese
- Powdered sugar

Sift the flour onto a clean work surface or into a large bowl. Dot with the butter. Make a well in the center and add the sugar, egg yolk, salt, and lemon zest. Working from the center outward, quickly knead all of the ingredients into a smooth dough. Press into a ball, wrap in foil or plastic wrap, and refrigerate for 2 hours.

Heat the oven to 375° and grease 2 cookie sheets. On a floured surface, roll out the dough to make 2 10-inch rounds. Place them on the cookie sheets, and pierce one of them all over with a fork, to keep it from rising unevenly during cooking. Bake for 8 to 10 minutes, until golden brown. While still warm, cut the pierced round into 16 wedges. Let cool on a rack with the other round.

To make the filling, put the milk, granulated sugar, salt, lemon zest, and egg yolks in the top of a double boiler over simmering water. Heat gently, stirring constantly, until smooth and slightly thickened. Remove the lemon custard from the heat and transfer to a mixing bowl. In a small saucepan, dissolve the gelatin in 3 tablespoons water over low heat. Stir into the lemon custard; let cool. Whip the cream until stiff. Beat the cream cheese to soften it. When the custard begins to set, stir in the cream cheese. Put the mixture in a blender and process until smooth. Return it to the bowl and carefully fold in the whipped cream.

Line the sides of a 10-inch springform pan with a strip of wax paper and place the whole shortbread round in it. Spoon in the cream cheese filling and smooth the surface. Arrange the shortbread wedges on top to form a round. Refrigerate until set. Remove the cheesecake from the pan and carefully peel away the wax paper. Sift powdered sugar on top.

Serves 16

GRAPE CHEESECAKE

Cake

- 4 eggs, separated
- 3 tablespoons lukewarm water
- 2/3 cup sugar
- 1 cup sifted flour
- Scant 1/2 cup sifted cornstarch
- 1 teaspoon baking powder

Filling and Topping

- 1 pound cream cheese
- 2 egg yolks
- 2/3 cup sugar
- Juice of 1 lemon
- 1 envelope unflavored gelatin, softened in cold water
- 1 cup heavy cream
- 8 ounces black grapes, halved and seeded
- 4 ounces seedless green grapes, halved
- 1/2 cup grape jelly
- 1 cup toasted sliced almonds

Butter the bottom and sides of a 9-inch springform pan. Heat the oven to 375°. Beat the egg yolks, water, and half of the sugar in a large bowl until pale and creamy. Beat the egg whites until stiff; fold in the remaining sugar. Fold into the egg yolk mixture. Sift together the flour, cornstarch, and baking powder. Fold into the egg mixture. Pour into the springform pan and bake for 40 minutes, or until a toothpick inserted in the center comes out clean. Let cool on a rack for 2 hours.

To make the filling, beat the cream cheese, egg yolks, sugar, and lemon juice. Dissolve the gelatin in 2 tablespoons water over low heat. Let cool slightly. Whip the cream until stiff and fold it into the cheese mixture, along with the gelatin. Cut the cake into 2 layers. Fill with half of the cream cheese mixture, top with the other layer, and spread the rest of the filling over the top and sides of the cake. Arrange the grapes on top in any design you like. Warm the jelly and drizzle it over the black grapes. Press almonds onto the sides of the cake and refrigerate to chill.

Serves 16

PEAR CHEESECAKE

Praline

- 3/4 cup sugar
- 3/4 cup coarsely chopped almonds

Pastry

- 1 1/4 cups sifted flour
- Pinch of salt
- 7 tablespoons butter, cut into small pieces
- 3 tablespoons sugar
- Few drops of vanilla extract
- 1/2 beaten egg

Filling

- 1 1-pound can pear halves, undrained
- 1/4 cup kirsch
- 9 ounces cream cheese
- 1/2 cup plus 2 tablespoons sugar
- Juice of 1 lemon
- 1 envelope unflavored gelatin, softened in cold water
- 1 cup heavy cream
- 1/3 cup red currant jelly

Heat the sugar and almonds in a medium saucepan over low heat. When the sugar has dissolved, boil slowly until golden. Pour the mixture onto an oiled cookie sheet and let it set. When cooled, crush the praline with a rolling pin and set aside.

To make the pastry, sift the flour and salt into a mixing bowl. Using a pastry blender, cut in the butter evenly. Mix in the sugar, vanilla extract, and egg to make a dough. Wrap in foil or plastic wrap and refrigerate for 2 hours.

Heat the oven to 400°. On a floured surface, roll out the dough to fit an 8-inch flan pan with a removable bottom. Place the dough in the pan and pierce it at close intervals. Cover with a sheet of baking foil or regular foil and weight it with dried beans. Bake for 30 minutes or so, until golden. Let cool on a rack.

To make the filling, drain the pears and reserve 3 tablespoons of the juice. Moisten the pears with a little kirsch. Beat the cream cheese, 1/2 cup sugar, lemon juice, and remaining kirsch in a medium-size bowl. Dissolve the gelatin in the reserved pear juice over low heat. Let cool slightly and stir into the cheese mixture. Refrigerate. Whip the cream with the remaining 2 tablespoons sugar. Mix two thirds of the whipped cream with 3 tablespoons praline and half of the jelly. Spread over the cheesecake. Fill a pastry tube with a star tip with the remaining whipped cream and decorate with rosettes. Decorate with the remaining jelly, heated, and garnish with 1 tablespoon praline. Refrigerate until ready to serve.

Serves 16

FRENCH CREAM CHEESE CAKE

Crust

1 cup graham cracker crumbs
4 tablespoons melted butter
4 tablespoons sugar
1/8 teaspoon cinnamon

Filling

1 pound cream cheese
4 eggs, separated
1/2 cup sugar
1 1/2 teaspoons vanilla extract
1 cup sour cream

Mix all of the crust ingredients, press into a 10-inch pie pan, and chill.

Mix the cream cheese and egg yolks and beat until well mixed and light. Add 1/4 cup sugar and 1/2 teaspoon vanilla extract. Beat again. Beat the egg whites separately until stiff. Fold into the cheese mixture and pour into the pie shell. Bake in a preheated 350° oven for 25 to 30 minutes. Let cool, then top with a mixture of the sour cream and the remaining sugar and vanilla extract. Bake at 450° for 5 minutes.

Makes 1 10-inch cake

My own, and a favorite.

JEFF BROOKS'S CHEESECAKES

3 pounds cream cheese
3/4 cup plus 1 tablespoon sugar
7 eggs
1/3 cup cornstarch
Dash of lemon extract
Dash of vanilla extract
2 tablespoons cognac
2 9-inch graham cracker pie shells (double the preceding recipe) pressed into 2 9-inch springform pans

Heat the oven to 300°. Whip the cream cheese until smooth. Add the sugar, eggs, cornstarch, extracts, and cognac. Strain it to get out all the lumps, or blend in a food processor until smooth. Pour into the pie shells. Set a pan of boiling-hot water in the bottom of the oven, and put the springform pans over it. Bake for 2 hours. Take the sides off the springform pans and let the cheesecakes cool on a rack before removing the pan bottoms.

Makes 2 9-inch cheesecakes

Variations: Top with a fruit glaze or a mixture of sour cream and sugar to taste, then cooked cut-up fruit, or just use the fruit. Also good is plain whipped cream.

CHEESECAKE IN A REGULAR PIE CRUST

- 1 tablespoon flour
- 1/2 cup sugar
- 8 ounces cream cheese
- 2 eggs
- 1/2 cup light cream
- 1/2 teaspoon vanilla extract
- 1/8 teaspoon lemon juice
- 1 8-inch pie shell (page 185)

Combine the flour and sugar and work in the cream cheese. Beat in the eggs, one at a time. Gradually stir in the cream and add the vanilla extract and lemon juice. Partially bake the pie shell; while it is still slightly warm, pour in the mixture and cover the exposed crust with foil. Bake in a preheated 350° oven for 40 to 50 minutes. Let cool, and top with your favorite topping.

Makes 1 8-inch cheesecake

ITALIAN CHEESECAKE

- 1 pound cream cheese
- 1 pound ricotta cheese
- 1½ cups sugar
- 4 eggs, slightly beaten
- 3 tablespoons cornstarch
- 3 tablespoons flour
- 1 teaspoon vanilla extract
- 1½ teaspoons lemon juice
- Grated zest of 1 lemon
- 1 pint sour cream
- 8 tablespoons melted butter (1 stick)

Heat the oven to 325°. Mix the cream cheese and ricotta. Add the sugar and mix well. Add the eggs, then the cornstarch, flour, vanilla extract, and lemon juice and zest. Add the sour cream and melted butter and mix. Pour the batter into a buttered 9-inch springform pan and bake for 1 hour, or until the cake is set in the center. Turn off the heat and leave the cake in the oven for 2 hours more. Remove and let cool at room temperature.

Makes 1 9-inch cheesecake

TORTE DI RICOTTA

- ½ cup toasted almonds
- 1½ pounds ricotta cheese
- 1 tablespoon chopped citron
- 4 eggs
- ⅓ cup granulated sugar
- 1 teaspoon vanilla extract
- 1 9-inch partially baked pie shell plus pie crust for lattice top (page 185)
- 2 tablespoons powdered sugar

Finely chop the almonds; add the ricotta and citron and mix thoroughly. Beat the eggs and granulated sugar well; add the vanilla extract. Add to the ricotta and stir until well blended and smooth. Pour the filling into the pie shell and place latticework strips over the top. Wet the edges and pinch them together; cover them with foil to prevent burning. Bake in a preheated 360° to 375° oven for 45 minutes, or until the mixture is firm but not dry to the touch and the pie crust is golden brown. Remove from the oven and let cool. Sprinkle with powdered sugar.

Serves 10 to 12

SOUR CREAM CHEESECAKE

- 2 sticks (1 cup) butter, at room temperature
- 2 3/4 cups sugar
- 6 eggs, at room temperature
- 3 cups sifted flour
- 1/2 teaspoon salt
- 1/4 teaspoon baking soda
- 3/4 cup sour cream
- 1/2 cup cream cheese
- 12 teaspoons vanilla extract

*H*eat the oven to 350°. Butter and flour a 10-inch tube pan. Cream the butter and sugar, using an electric mixer. Add the eggs, one at a time, beating well after each addition. Sift the flour with the salt and baking soda, and add to the butter mixture in three batches, alternating with the sour cream and cream cheese and mixing well after each addition. Blend in the vanilla extract. Pour the batter into the pan and bake for about 1 1/4 hours, until the top is light brown and a tester inserted near the center comes out clean. Let cool in the pan.

Makes 1 10-inch cheesecake

LOW-CALORIE CHEESECAKE

- 1 teaspoon butter
- 2 tablespoons bread crumbs
- 3 1/2 cups cottage cheese
- 1/2 cup sifted cornstarch
- 1/2 cup plus 2 tablespoons sugar
- 2 teaspoons vanilla extract
- 1 tablespoon grated lemon zest
- 4 large eggs, separated

Heat the oven to 350°. Lightly butter the sides and bottom of a 9-inch springform pan. Press the bread crumbs smoothly over the bottom of pan to line it. In an electric mixer, beat the cottage cheese, cornstarch, 1/2 cup sugar, vanilla extract, lemon zest, and egg yolks until smooth. In another bowl, beat the egg whites until they peak; add the 2 tablespoons sugar, a little at a time. Fold the egg whites into the other mixture, then pour into the pan and bake for 55 minutes. Turn off the oven and leave the cake in it for another hour. Take it out and let cool on a rack. Do not chill it. Cut into quarters and serve as is or with a fruit topping made without sugar.

Makes 1 9-inch cheesecake

Cookies

*M*ost people have cookie thieves at home, and I honestly believe many of us make cookies just to enjoy catching them. We seem to have a voracious appetite for them, too. For pure enjoyment, these recipes are at the top of the list.

CHERRY AND SESAME COOKIES

- 2 sticks (1 cup) butter
- 1/4 cup sugar
- 1 teaspoon almond extract
- 2 cups flour
- 1/4 teaspoon salt
- Sesame seeds
- 1/3 cup halved candied cherries

In a mixing bowl, cream the butter and sugar until light and fluffy. Add the almond extract, flour, and salt. Beat until just mixed. Refrigerate to chill. Shape into 1-inch balls, roll in sesame seeds, press a cherry half on top, and bake on greased cookie sheets in a preheated 400° oven for about 10 minutes. Let them sit in the oven for another 2 to 3 minutes, then put them on a rack to cool.

Makes 3 dozen

HERMITS

- 1/2 cup shortening
- 2 eggs
- 1/2 cup plus 2 tablespoons sugar
- 2/3 cup molasses
- 1 3/4 cups flour
- 1 1/2 teaspoons cinnamon
- 3/4 teaspoon ginger
- 3/4 teaspoon baking soda
- 1/2 teaspoon salt
- 1/2 cup seedless raisins
- 1/2 cup chopped walnuts or pecans

In an electric mixing bowl, cream the shortening, 1 egg, and the 1/2 cup sugar. Add the molasses and beat until fluffy. In another bowl combine the dry ingredients. Add them to the creamed mixture. Fold in the raisins and nuts. Divide into 2 portions, transfer to a greased cookie sheet, and shape into 2 12 × 2-inch rectangles. Bake in a preheated 360° oven for about 15 minutes, then take them out and brush them with a glaze made from the remaining egg and sugar, beaten together. Cut into bars while still warm and let cool on a rack.

Makes 3 dozen

BANANA GRANOLA COOKIES

- 1/2 cup shortening
- 1 cup brown sugar
- 1 1/2 cups flour
- 1 egg
- 1/2 teaspoon vanilla extract
- 3 ripe bananas, well mashed
- 1 teaspoon cinnamon
- 1/2 teaspoon salt
- 1/2 teaspoon baking soda
- 1 cup granola

In a blender, mix the shortening and sugar. Add the flour, egg, vanilla extract, and bananas. Blend well. Add the cinnamon, salt, and baking soda. Blend again. Stir in the granola. Drop onto greased cookie sheets by the teaspoonful. Bake in a preheated 360° to 375° oven for about 12 minutes. Let cool on a rack.

Makes about 48

CHOCOLATE CHIP DROP COOKIES

- 2 sticks (1 cup) butter, softened
- 1 cup brown sugar
- 1 cup granulated (white) sugar
- 2 eggs
- 1 teaspoon vanilla extract
- 2 cups plus 4 tablespoons sifted flour
- 1 teaspoon salt
- 1 1/2 teaspoons baking soda
- 1 cup chopped walnuts, pecans, and/or almonds
- 1 cup chocolate chips

Cream the butter and gradually add the sugars; heat in a saucepan until creamy. Transfer to a mixing bowl and beat in the eggs and vanilla extract. Sift together the dry ingredients and stir into the butter mixture. Stir in the nuts and chocolate and mix well. Drop by the tablespoonful onto greased cookie sheets and bake in a preheated 375° oven until slightly browned. The centers should still be soft.

Makes 24 to 30

MERINGUE CUPS

- 3 egg whites, at room temperature
- 1 cup sugar
- 6 ounces unsweetened chocolate, melted
- 1/2 teaspoon vanilla extract

Heat the oven to 350°. Grease 2 cookie sheets with clarified butter and set aside. In a mixing bowl, beat the egg whites to the soft-peaks stage. Add the sugar, a little at a time, and beat until stiff. Fold in the chocolate and vanilla extract. Shape the meringue into cups on the cookie sheets and bake for at least 15 minutes. Let cool on a rack.

To use, set them on dessert dishes, fill with fresh fruit, and top with a nice rich brandied cream sauce (page 260).

Makes 4 to 6

OTHER DESSERTS

FRIED DOUGH

- 6 cups lukewarm milk (100°)
- 6 tablespoons granulated sugar
- 2 teaspoons salt
- 2 compressed yeast cakes, crumbled
- 4 eggs
- 6 tablespoons shortening
- 7 cups sifted flour
- Fat for deep-frying
- Nutmeg
- Powdered sugar

Mix the milk, granulated sugar, and salt. Add the yeast, then stir in the eggs and shortening. Mix in the flour, using your hand to blend it well. Knead for at least 10 to 15 minutes. Set it aside, covered, to rise until doubled in bulk. Punch it down and let it rise again. Make a ball out of it, and set it aside to rest and rise a bit more, 15 minutes or so. Cut the pieces to whatever size and shape you wish and deep-fry them in 375° fat, turning them once the underside has browned to your satisfaction. When they are fully cooked, do as the Amish do—mix a bit of nutmeg with powdered sugar and sprinkle it on the hot dough as soon as it comes out of the fat. I love to eat them just as they are, but you can put anything on yours, so long as you enjoy.

Makes 18 pieces

Many of us go for the tasty, fabulous-smelling fried dough often seen on stands at a fair or in the window of a specialty restaurant. They are all really great and I find no fault with any of them, but I can honestly say that this recipe, which I begged *for in the Amish country of Pennsylvania, is something to behold.*

CALAS TOUT CHAUDS

- 2 cups cooked rice
- 3 eggs, well beaten
- 1/2 teaspoon vanilla extract
- 1 teaspoon granulated sugar
- 1/4 teaspoon salt
- 6 tablespoons flour
- 3 teaspoons baking powder
- Fat for deep-frying
- Sifted confectioner's sugar

Combine the rice, eggs, and vanilla extract and mix thoroughly. Stir in the granulated sugar, salt, flour, and baking powder. Drop into hot (360°) deep fat by the spoonful and fry until golden brown. Drain on absorbent paper, sprinkle with confectioner's sugar, and serve very hot.

Makes 18 fritters

CREOLE PRALINES

- 3 cups sugar
- 1 cup light cream or rich milk
- 1 teaspoon vanilla extract
- 2 1/2 cups pecans or mixed pecans and black walnuts
- Dash of salt

In a heavy skillet, cook the sugar with 2 to 3 tablespoons water until caramelized. In a large saucepan, heat the cream to a simmer. Carefully pour in the caramel and cook, stirring with a long-handled spoon, until a small amount dropped into cold water forms a soft ball (236° on a candy thermometer). Remove from the heat and let cool to lukewarm. Add the vanilla extract, nuts, and salt, and beat until stiff and creamy. Drop onto a buttered cookie sheet and let cool.

Makes about 20 3-inchers

CARAMEL BUTTERCREAM WITH PECAN PRALINE

Praline

- 1 1/2 cups shelled pecans
- 1 cup sugar
- 1/2 cup water

Buttercream

- 4 sticks (1 cup) unsalted butter, softened
- 1 cup sugar
- 1/2 cup plus 2 tablespoons water
- 10 egg yolks

Toast the nuts in a preheated 375° oven until lightly browned, about 5 to 6 minutes. In a heavy 1 1/2- to 2-quart saucepan, dissolve the sugar in the water over medium heat, stirring. Boil without stirring until the syrup turns a light caramel color, 6 to 8 minutes. Add the nuts and stir with a wooden spoon until they are completely covered with caramel and begin to make a popping sound, 2 to 3 minutes. Immediately pour onto a well-oiled heavy tray or marble surface and spread out as rapidly as possible. When hardened, about 10 minutes or so, break into pieces and grind in a food processor to make a powder. Be careful not to grind it too much or it will turn to paste.

In a large bowl, cream the butter until light and fluffy. Set aside. In a heavy 2- to 3-quart saucepan over low heat, dissolve the sugar in the 1/2 cup water, stirring. Bring to a boil and boil without stirring until the syrup turns an amber caramel color, 6 to 8 minutes. Brush down any sugar crystals on the sides of the pan with a heavy brush dipped in cold water. Remove from the heat and let cool for 1 minute.

In the large bowl of an electric mixer, beat the egg yolks until fluffy and lemon-colored. When syrup has cooled for 1 minute, tip the pan away from you, to avoid spattering, and carefully add the remaining 2 tablespoons water. With the mixer on high speed, very slowly pour the caramel syrup down the sides of the bowl, into the egg yolks. (Be careful not to pour onto the beater, or the syrup will spatter.) Continue beating at high speed until cool, about 5 to 7 minutes. Gradually beat in the creamed butter. Add the praline and combine thoroughly. Refrigerate until thick, about 30 minutes. Serve as is or use as a pie filling.

Makes about 4 cups

Caramel is sugar cooked until it is one step short of being burned. It is both simpler and more delicate than it appears and can be mastered easily. While expert chefs can simply cook sugar in a pan or skillet until it turns to caramel—which happens in the blink of an eye—most cooks add water to the sugar to give themselves some leeway in coping with sugar's otherwise treacherous temperament. As the sugar cooks, the water evaporates and the sugar progresses through several stages: soft ball (234° to 240°), hard ball (250° to 268°), soft crack (270° to 290°), hard crack (300° to 310°), and finally caramel (320° to 338°), when it turns from clear honey to amber in color. As soon as the bubbles become large and close together, watch it very carefully or the syrup will burn.

Cold Soufflés and Mousses

LEMON SOUFFLÉ

3 eggs, separated
Scant 1/2 cup superfine (castor) sugar
Juice and finely grated zest of 2 lemons

1 1/2 tablespoons unflavored gelatin, softened in cold water
1/4 pint double or heavy cream
Chopped nuts

Lightly butter a 1-pint soufflé dish. Cut a strip of greaseproof paper, twice the height of the dish plus 3 inches, and long enough to go around it. Fold down the 3 inches, butter the strip just made, and tie the paper, buttered side in around the outside of the dish.

Put the egg yolks, sugar, and lemon juice and zest in a heatproof mixing bowl. Set the bowl over a pan of hot water and whisk until the mixture is thickened and creamy. Remove from the heat and whisk to cool it. Dissolve the gelatin in 3 tablespoons hot water and whisk into the egg mixture. Whip the cream to the soft-peaks stage and fold it in. Cool by whisking or refrigeration.

Whisk the egg whites to the stiff-peaks stage. When the cream mixture is just about to set, fold in the egg whites. Pour into the soufflé dish and refrigerate until firmly set. Carefully ease the paper away from the soufflé with the back of a knife. Decorate with chopped nuts pressed around the sides and rosettes of whipped cream on top. Serve as soon as possible.

Serves 4

Variations: Apricot Soufflé. Omit the lemon juice and zest; instead use 1/2 cup apricot purée and the juice of 1/2 lemon. Add them after cooking and cooling the egg yolks and sugar.

Strawberry Soufflé. Omit the lemon juice and zest; use 1/2 cup strawberry purée.

ORANGE SOUFFLÉ

- 2 envelopes unflavored gelatin
- 1 cup cold water
- 8 eggs, separated
- 2 6-ounce cans frozen orange juice concentrate, thawed
- 1 cup plus 3 tablespoons sugar
- 1½ cups heavy cream, chilled

Sprinkle the gelatin in the cold water and let it soften for about 5 minutes. Meanwhile, beat the egg yolks with a whisk or electric beater until they are thick and yellow. Beat in the gelatin. Cook the mixture in a small enameled or stainless-steel saucepan over moderate heat, stirring constantly, until thickened enough to lightly coat a spoon. Do not let it come to a boil or it will curdle. Take the pan off the heat and quickly stir in the orange juice concentrate. Transfer the mixture to a large bowl and refrigerate for about half an hour, until it has thickened to a syrupy consistency.

Beat the egg whites until they begin to froth, then slowly pour in 1 cup sugar and beat until the whites form stiff peaks on the beater blades. In another bowl, whip 1 cup cream until it holds its shape softly, then beat into it the remaining 3 tablespoons sugar. With a rubber spatula, gently fold the whipped cream into the orange mixture, mixing thoroughly. (If the mixture has set too firmly and formed lumps, first beat it gently with a whisk or rotary beater.) Fold in the egg whites until no streaks of white show. Tie a piece of paper around a 1½-quart soufflé dish, about 2 inches or so above the top of the dish. Pour the mixture into it and smooth the top with a rubber spatula. Refrigerate until firm, about 4 hours. Remove the paper collar and garnish the top of the soufflé with the remaining cream, whipped and forced through a pastry bag to make rosettes in any pattern you desire.

Serves 4

STRAWBERRY SOUFFLÉ

- 2 pints fresh strawberries
- 2 envelopes unflavored gelatin, softened in cold water
- 3/4 cup sugar
- 1/2 cup water
- 1 tablespoon lemon juice
- 2 tablespoons kirsch
- 3 egg whites
- 1 cup heavy cream

Cut a 6 × 30-inch strip of parchment paper or brown paper bag and brush one side with oil or melted butter. Tape the paper, oiled side in, around the top of a 1-quart soufflé dish.

Wash and hull the strawberries. Reserve a dozen, and purée the rest in a food processor or blender. Mix the gelatin with 1/2 cup sugar in a saucepan. Stir in the water and cook over low heat, stirring, until the gelatin dissolves. Pour into a bowl and mix in the strawberry purée, lemon juice, and kirsch. Refrigerate, but give it a stir frequently, until the mixture thickens slightly. This should take about half an hour and is really crucial to making the soufflé thick enough to stand up.

Beat the egg whites until frothy, add the remaining 1/4 cup sugar, and beat until stiff. Fold into the strawberry mixture. Whip the cream until stiff and fold it in. *Gently* pour the mixture into the soufflé dish. Refrigerate until firm, about 4 hours. To serve, carefully remove the paper, so as not to rip the outside of the mounded soufflé, and garnish with the reserved whole strawberries.

Serves 4

This is called a soufflé, and looks like one, but it is not cooked.

RHUBARB SOUFFLÉ

- 1/2 cup red currant jelly
- 2 tablespoons granulated sugar
- 1 pound fresh or thawed frozen rhubarb, chopped
- 1 envelope unflavored gelatin softened in 2 tablespoons cold water
- Shortening
- 4 egg whites

- 1 cup heavy cream
- 1 teaspoon vanilla extract

In a 2- to 3-quart saucepan, stir the jelly with 1 tablespoon sugar over moderate heat until melted. Add the rhubarb, cover, and cook for 5 minutes. Increase the heat to moderately high and cook for 5 to 10 minutes, stirring several times, until tender. Strain into a 1-quart saucepan and let drain for a few minutes. Cook the liquid over moderate heat for 4 to 6 minutes, until only 1/2 cup remains, and purée the rhubarb in a food processor. Remove the rhubarb liquid from the heat and stir in the gelatin. Let cool to room temperature and stir in the purée.

Cut a 3-inch piece of wax paper long enough to go all the way around a soufflé dish. Apply a film of solid shortening to the paper and tie it around the dish. In a medium-size bowl, beat the egg whites until soft peaks hold when the beater is lifted. Sprinkle with the remaining tablespoon of sugar and beat for a few seconds. In another bowl, beat the cream and vanilla extract until soft peaks form. Fold the whipped cream into the rhubarb and then gently but thoroughly fold in the beaten egg whites. Pour into the soufflé dish and smooth the surface. Refrigerate for at least 3 to 4 hours.

Serves 8

CHOCOLATE MOUSSE

- 4 ounces semisweet chocolate
- 1 1/3 tablespoons water
- 4 eggs, separated
- Whipped cream

Break the chocolate into small pieces and put in a small heatproof bowl with the water. Set over hot water until the chocolate has melted. Stir it until smooth. Add the egg yolks, stir well, and let cool. Whisk the egg whites until stiff enough to stand in peaks, then fold into the chocolate mixture. Make sure the mousse is perfectly smooth. Pour it into dessert dishes and refrigerate until set. Decorate it with rosettes of whipped cream.

Serves 4

VENETIAN CHOCOLATE MOUSSE

- 4 ounces semisweet chocolate
- 8 tablespoons (1 stick) butter
- 1 teaspoon vanilla extract
- 4 tablespoons Cointreau
- 2 tablespoons brewed strong coffee
- 4 eggs, separated, plus 6 egg whites (10 whites in all), at room temperature
- 1/2 cup plus sugar
- Pinch of cream of tartar
- Whipped cream

In the top of a double boiler set over simmering water, melt and mix the chocolate and butter. Add the vanilla extract, Cointreau, and coffee. Scrape into a bowl and set aside. Wash and dry the double boiler and in it beat together and cook the egg yolks and 1/2 cup sugar for 6 to 8 minutes, until smooth, creamy, and thick. Set the double boiler top on a pan of crushed ice and whisk to cool quickly. In a mixing bowl, beat the egg whites, cream of tartar, and a little sugar until very stiff.

Mix the yolk mixture into the chocolate sauce, then mix in half of the egg whites; fold in the remaining half. Spoon into stemmed champagne or soufflé glasses, chill, and serve with whipped cream on top.

Serves 4

This recipe was the result of an error in the kitchen—an assistant added twice the amount of egg whites called for. It is my favorite chocolate mousse, smooth and light.

Custard and Pudding

SOFT CUSTARD

2 cups milk
4 egg yolks, beaten
1/4 cup sugar
Large pinch of salt
1 teaspoon maple or vanilla extract

Scald the milk, then pour it into the top of a double boiler set over boiling water and mix in the egg yolks, sugar, and salt. Stir with a wooden spoon until it begins to get thick. Set it aside and let cool, then add the extract and chill.

Serves 4

BAKED CUSTARD

2 cups milk
2 pinches of salt
2 eggs plus 2 egg whites
Large sprinkling of nutmeg
1/2 cup sugar
1 teaspoon vanilla extract

Blend the milk, sugar, and salt. Beat the eggs and extra whites and add to the milk mixture. Add the vanilla extract and pour into custard cups or molds. Set them in a pan of hot water and bake in a preheated 325° oven for an hour or more. Test one for doneness: insert a small, thin knife blade into the custard and pull it out. If it comes out clean, the custard is done. If any custard shows on the blade, it is not.

Serves 4

Variation: Caramel Custard. Heat 1 cup sugar in a heavy pan over very low heat and add 1 tablespoon water. Stir continuously with a wooden spoon for about 10 minutes, until the sugar is completely melted. Remove it from the heat and *very slowly* (so as not to get splashed) stir in about 1/4 cup boiling-hot water. Pour enough of the syrup into each custard cup to fill the bottom and swirl it around the inside. Pour the cooled custard over this and bake. To serve, swirl the cups in hot water for a few seconds, invert onto a serving dish, and let the caramel pour over the custard.

BAVARIAN CREAM

- 5 eggs, beaten
- 1/2 cup sugar
- 2 tablespoons unflavored gelatin softened in 1/4 cup cold water
- 2 cups heavy cream
- 1 teaspoon vanilla extract
- 1 teaspoon Grand Marnier

In the top of a double boiler set over simmering water, heat the eggs until an instant-read thermometer registers 80° to 85°. Using a hand-held mixer at medium speed, beat for 5 to 6 minutes. Beat in half of the sugar. Take off the heat, beat in the remaining sugar, and continue to beat until the mixture forms soft peaks. Fold in the gelatin and refrigerate until chilled.

In a chilled bowl (or a bowl set over a basin of crushed ice), whip the cream to the soft-peaks stage; do not overbeat. Add the vanilla extract and Grand Marnier and beat until the cream is a little firmer. Fold it into the egg mixture and chill.

Serves 10

The amount of gelatin suggested produces a sturdy consistency for puff pastry desserts like cream slices and napoleons. If you intend to serve Bavarian cream as a pudding, use less gelatin, to make it softer.

RICE PUDDING

- 1 1/3 cups milk
- Large pinch of salt
- 1 tablespoon butter
- 6 tablespoons sugar
- 4 eggs
- 1 teaspoon vanilla extract
- 2 cups cooled cooked rice
- 1/2 cup raisins
- 1 teaspoon lemon juice

Beat together the milk, salt, butter, sugar, eggs, and vanilla extract. Mix with the rice, raisins, and lemon juice, place in a buttered casserole dish, and bake at 325° for about 45 minutes.

Serves 6

Variation: White House Rice Pudding. F.D.R. started the tradition of serving rice pudding at the White House, and it has continued with various recipes. First off, substitute crushed pineapple for the raisins and add a bit more milk or cream. John F. Kennedy loved rice pudding with currants. Lyndon B. Johnson had to have *big* chunks of pineapple. Jimmy Carter loved crushed peanuts in his. Ronald Reagan loves jelly beans in his. (I cannot, in all honesty, say that the last is true.)

RICE PUDDING WITH MERINGUE

- 1/4 cup raw rice
- 1 cup water
- 2 cups milk
- 2 eggs, separated
- 1/8 teaspoon salt
- 7 tablespoons sugar
- 1 teaspoon vanilla extract

Cook the rice and water in the top of a double boiler set over boiling water for about half an hour, until the rice swells and is dry. Add the milk and continue to cook for 5 minutes or so. Beat the egg yolks with the salt and 3 tablespoons sugar. Pour in a little of the hot milk, mix well, and add to the rice mixture. Cook until creamy. Beat the egg whites and remaining 4 tablespoons sugar until stiff. Add the vanilla extract to the rice mixture, pour into a buttered baking dish, and top with the meringue. Bake in a preheated 325° oven for 15 to 20 minutes to brown the meringue. Chill well before serving.

Serves 6

COCONUT PUDDING

- 8 tablespoons (1 stick) butter
- 2 cups sugar
- 6 eggs
- 1 cup half-and-half
- 2 to 2½ cups grated coconut
- 1 teaspoon vanilla extract (optional)
- Heavy cream or whipped cream

Cream the butter and sugar. Beat in the eggs, one by one, then the half-and-half. Fold in the coconut. Add the vanilla. Pour into a buttered 2-quart baking dish and place in a preheated 375° oven. Now you must watch it. When the pudding begins to brown, turn the browned part in. Repeat this three to five times, as the pudding thickens. Finally, let the pudding come to a golden brown all over and remove it from the oven. Serve hot with cream, or cold with whipped cream.

Serves 8

REAL INDIAN PUDDING

- 1½ cups milk
- 2 tablespoons cornmeal
- ⅓ cup molasses
- 2 tablespoons butter
- ⅜ teaspoon salt
- ⅜ teaspoon ginger
- 3½ tablespoons sugar
- ½ well-beaten small egg
- ¼ cup raisins
- 2 large pinches cinnamon

In the top of a double boiler set over boiling water, bring the milk to a boil, stir in the cornmeal, and cook for 15 minutes. Stir in the molasses and cook for 5 minutes. Remove from the heat and stir in the remaining ingredients. Pour into a well-buttered baking dish or individual dishes and bake in a preheated 300° oven for 1½ to 2 hours. Use a toothpick to check for doneness. Serve hot or cold.

Serves 6

Note: If you want the pudding to have a soft center, add ¾ cup cold milk along with the final ingredients.

Fruit

CARAMEL PEARS IN PUFF PASTRY

- 1 quart water
- 2 cups sugar
- 1 vanilla bean
- Juice of 1 lemon
- 1 2-inch piece lemon zest
- 2 small firm ripe pears, peeled but not cored, and rubbed with lemon juice
- 1/2 pound puff pastry (page 183), rolled out 1/8 inch thick
- 1 egg, beaten with a pinch of salt
- 3/4 cup heavy cream
- 1/2 teaspoon vanilla extract
- 4 tablespoons almond praline (page 200)

In a 2- or 3-quart saucepan, combine the water, sugar, vanilla bean, and lemon juice and zest. Stir over medium-high heat until the sugar is dissolved. Bring to a boil, reduce the heat to a simmer, and add the pears. Poach them until just tender when pierced with a skewer, 20 to 25 minutes, and let cool in the syrup. Drain the pears, strain the syrup, and reserve both.

Cut the pastry into 4 rectangles, 4 × 2 1/2 inches each, and put them on a buttered heavy cookie sheet. Cut the remaining pastry into strips 1/2 inch wide by 4 inches long. Brush the edges of the rectangles with cold water and add strips lengthwise along two sides. Press slightly to seal them together. Prick the shells with a fork and refrigerate for at least 20 minutes. Brush the borders of the pastry with the beaten egg and bake on the middle rack of a preheated 375° oven until the pastry is puffed and golden, about 15 to 20 minutes.

In a 1- to 2-quart saucepan, boil the reserved syrup until it begins to caramelize and turn a rich golden color, about 15 minutes. You will have approximately 1 cup of reduced glaze. While the glaze is still warm, brush it on the bottom of the pastry to seal it.

In a large bowl, whip the cream until it is firm. Fold in the vanilla extract and 3 tablespoons praline powder and set aside. Cut the pears in half, scoop out the cores, and trim to fit the pastry, if necessary. Cut crosswise into 1/4-inch-thick slices.

Press with the palm of your hand to fan them out slightly. Spread each pastry shell with about 1/4 inch praline cream and top with a fanned pear half. Brush the pears with more warm glaze and sprinkle with the remaining praline.

Serves 4

MARTIN YAN'S CHOCOLATE PEARS

- 2 pears
- 1 1/4 cups sugar
- 2 pinches of salt
- 3 tablespoons cornstarch
- 1/2 cup Chinese rice wine
- 2 pints boiling water
- 2 egg yolks
- 1 3/4 sticks (7/8 cup) butter
- 1 teaspoon vanilla extract
- 8 ounces dark, semisweet, or sweet chocolate

Peel and core the pears. In a saucepan, mix half the sugar with the salt, cornstarch, and half the wine. Whisk in the boiling water and poach the pears over low heat for 7 to 8 minutes. Remove them, cut in half, and set aside.

Beat the egg yolks with the remaining sugar and wine, and pour slowly into the sugar syrup. Cook for a few minutes. Remove from the heat and whisk in 1 1/4 sticks butter and the vanilla extract. Ladle into the bottom of 2 dessert dishes with a well. Place the pears upside down in the center of the custard.

Melt the chocolate with the remaining 4 tablespoons butter, to keep it from hardening too much. Fill the pear cores with the chocolate and refrigerate. Turn the pears right side up, set them back on the custard, and streak designs down the sides with the remaining melted chocolate.

Serves 2

POACHED PEARS WITH SABAYON

- 4 pears, cored and halved
- 1/2 cup sugar
- 4 jiggers brandy or liqueur

Sabayon

- 8 egg yolks
- 8 tablespoons Marsala
- 3/4 cup sugar
- 2 to 4 tablespoons brandy or liqueur

- Spongecake
- Ice cream

Poach the pears in 2 quarts water with the sugar and brandy. Drain and let cool. Put the egg yolks, Marsala, sugar, and brandy in a mixing bowl (or the top of a large double boiler) and set over boiling water (not *in* it). Whisk until it becomes thick and mousselike. Place a slice of spongecake on each dessert plate, put a small scoop of ice cream on it, and set a pear half on that, cavity down. Top with sabayon.

Serves 4

This dessert can be served warm, just after you have cooked it, or chilled.

HAWAIIAN MELBA PEARS

- 4 scoops ice cream
- Spongecake, sliced
- 1 1-pound 10-ounce can pear halves (6 to 8 halves), drained
- 2 tablespoons butter
- 1 tablespoon brown sugar
- 1 tablespoon sliced toasted almonds
- 1 1/3 tablespoons Cointreau
- 1/3 cup dark rum

Mound scoops of ice cream on slices of spongecake. In a large saucepan, sauté the pear halves in butter and sugar. Add the almonds, Cointreau, and rum, and flame it. Place the pear halves over the ice cream and serve.

Serves 4

MIXED-FRUIT GELATIN SALAD

Fruit Mold

1 envelope unflavored gelatin
2 cups cut-up soft fruit (peaches, strawberries, blueberries, etc.)
1 tablespoon lemon juice

Topping

1 cup whipped cream
2 tablespoons mayonnaise
2 tablespoons brandy

Mix the gelatin in the mold according to the package directions. Add the fruit and lemon juice and refrigerate until firm; unmold onto a serving plate. Combine the whipped cream, mayonnaise, and brandy and spoon over the salad.

Serves 4

HOT FROZEN SURPRISE CAKE

1 poundcake
1 quart ice cream
3 cups mixed cut-up fruit
2 tablespoons butter
1 cup brandy

Cut the poundcake into 3 slices lengthwise and fill the layers with ice cream. Put it in the freezer. Sauté the fruit in the butter and brandy. To serve, cut a slice of cake and ladle cooked fruit over it.

Serves 6

STUFFED ORANGES

- 4 oranges
- 1/3 cup pitted dates cut into small pieces
- 1/3 cup chopped pecans
- 1/3 cup shredded coconut
- White of 1 small egg
- 1/3 cup superfine sugar

Cut a thin slice from one end of each orange so that the pulp is exposed. From the other end cut a fine sliver so the oranges will stand securely upright. Carefully scoop out all of the orange pulp, and discard the pith and seeds. Cut up the pulp and combine it with the dates, nuts, and coconut. Fill the shells with this mixture. Beat the egg white until nearly stiff, then gradually beat in the sugar. When stiff, spread a spoonful of the meringue over the top of each orange. Place in a baking pan and brown in a preheated 350° oven.

Serves 4

AMBROSIA

- 3 medium oranges
- 2 ripe bananas, sliced
- 1 1/2 cups grated coconut
- 2 to 3 tablespoons sugar
- Lemon juice to taste
- Ripe strawberries (optional)
- Fresh pineapple slices or chunks (optional)

Peel the oranges and slice them crosswise; remove the seeds. Arrange the oranges, bananas, and coconut in layers in a deep glass bowl. Sprinkle each layer with sugar and lemon juice. End with the coconut on top. Let stand for at least 2 hours, preferably in the refrigerator. Add the strawberries and pineapple.

Serves 6

Variation: The addition of Triple Sec, Cointreau, or cognac to this old and original recipe from the Cajuns of Nova Scotia makes it something out of the ordinary.

BANANAS FORSTER

- 4 firm ripe bananas
- Banana or coconut extract
- Grated fresh coconut
- 2 tablespoons butter
- Triple Sec
- Brandy or Cointreau

Peel the bananas and moisten them with a small amount of extract. Roll them in the coconut. In a large skillet, heat the butter until it just begins to pop. Sauté the bananas in the butter until they just begin to turn a very light brown. Add the Triple Sec and brandy and heat through. Serve the juices from the pan over each. If you like, flambé it: pour on a jigger of 151 rum and light it.

Serves 4

FRESH FRUIT SALAD

Dressing

- 4 cups sugar
- 4 eggs, well beaten
- Juice and zest of 4 citrus fruits

- 1/4 watermelon
- 1/2 cantaloupe
- 2 bananas
- 1 bunch seedless grapes
- 1/4 box strawberries
- 1/2 pineapple
- Juice of 1/2 lime and 1/2 lemon
- 2 tablespoons butter
- 4 jiggers sweet sake

Combine the dressing ingredients in a saucepan and blend well. Cook over low to medium heat, stirring constantly, until the mixture comes to a boil. Boil for 1 minute. Remove from the heat, let cool, and refrigerate. Cut the fruit into large pieces, toss with the citrus juice, sauté in butter and sake, and serve in bowls with the dressing.

Serves 6 to 8

HAWAIIAN RICE SALAD

- 6 tablespoons heavy cream
- 1/4 cup sour cream
- 1 jigger rice wine
- 1/4 cup fresh coconut milk
- 3/4 cup chopped fresh pineapple
- 1/4 cup chopped almonds
- 1/4 cup grated fresh coconut
- 3 cups cooked rice
- 16 candied cherries, chopped
- Dash or 2 of salt

Whip the cream, add the sour cream, whip again, add the wine and coconut milk, and set aside. Mix all of the remaining ingredients, and serve the dressing on top.

Serves 4

PORCUPINES

- 2 cups shelled pecans
- 1 cup pitted dates
- 2 cups plus flaked coconut
- 1 firmly packed cup dark brown sugar
- 2 eggs

Finely grind the pecans and dates. Mix with the 2 cups coconut and the sugar and eggs. Shape the mixture into logs 4 inches long and 1/2 inch thick and roll them in more coconut. Put the logs on a lightly buttered cookie sheet and bake in a preheated 350° oven for 10 to 12 minutes.

Makes 36

Sherbet and Ice Cream

Sherbet is served between courses to make the meal more interesting by refreshing the taste buds. There was a time when fresh fruit was served to this end, but then came sherbet (or, as the fashionable say, sorbet).

ANY-FRUIT SHERBET

- 1 10-ounce package frozen fruit, thawed
- 1/2 cup sweet vermouth plus 2 tablespoons confectioner's sugar, or dry vermouth plus granulated sugar
- 1 cup heavy cream

Blend until frothy, pour into a container, and freeze. To serve, spoon into footed goblets.

Serves 4

ORANGE-LIME-APPLE SHERBET

- 1 lime, peeled and seeded
- 2 oranges, peeled and seeded
- 2 apples, peeled and cored
- 1/2 cup honey
- 1 cup milk
- 1 cup dry vermouth
- 1 cup each lime, orange, and apple juice

Purée all of the ingredients and freeze for at least 1 hour. Whip the mixture after it is frozen, and refreeze until ready to serve.

Serves 4

MELON SHERBET

- 1 melon
- 1 cup pineapple juice
- 1 cup dry vermouth
- Juice of 1 lime and 1/2 lemon
- 1/2 cup honey
- 1 kiwi fruit

Cut the melon in half, dig out the pulp, and whip it in a blender with the pineapple juice, vermouth, citrus juice, honey, and kiwi pulp. Blend until smooth. Fill the melon halves with it and freeze.

Serve between courses, as a palate refresher, or as a dessert, with whipped cream and pecans or walnuts over it.

Serves 4

STRAWBERRY CHAMPAGNE SHERBET

- 1 pint strawberries, washed and hulled
- 1 cup champagne
- 6 tablespoons confectioner's sugar
- 2 tablespoons melted chocolate or Hershey's liquid chocolate

Whip the strawberries, champagne, sugar, and chocolate. Freeze for at least 2 hours. Whip it again and serve in footed goblets, between the salad and main course.

Serves 4

Variation: If you find the sherbet too sweet for your taste, add a bit of fresh orange or lemon juice to it just before serving.

RASPBERRY SHERBET

- 1 package frozen raspberries, thawed
- 1 tablespoon frozen orange juice concentrate
- 1/4 cup sweet vermouth
- 1 tablespoon fresh lemon juice
- 1/2 cup sugar
- 1 egg white

Combine everything but the egg white in a blender and mix thoroughly. Whip the egg white to the soft-peaks stage and fold into the other mixture. Freeze and serve.

Serves 4

ORANGE SHERBET

- 1 cup sugar
- 1 12-ounce can frozen orange juice concentrate
- 2 ounces frozen lemon juice
- 1 cup corn syrup
- 1/2 cup dry vermouth
- Grated zest of 1 orange

Boil the sugar in about 4 cups water for 4 to 5 minutes. Add the remaining ingredients, mix, and freeze.

Serves 4

CRANBERRY-ORANGE-WINE SHERBET

- 1 cup whole cranberries
- 1 cup cranberry juice
- 1 6-ounce can frozen orange juice concentrate
- Pulp and grated zest of 1 orange
- 1 cup sweet vermouth
- Dash of cardamom
- 2 to 4 tablespoons milk

Mix the cranberries, cranberry juice, orange juice concentrate, orange pulp and zest, vermouth, cardamom, and 2 tablespoons milk. Check the color; if it is still rather dark, add another 2 tablespoons milk. Mix in a blender, pour into a large pan, and freeze for an hour or so. Whip it in the pan and refreeze.

Serves 4

MANGO ICE CREAM

- 1 1/4 cups mango purée (from 2 large mangoes)
- 1 cup heavy cream
- 3 tablespoons lime juice
- 1/2 cup honey
- 8 ounces plain yogurt
- 2 tablespoons amber rum

In a large bowl, combine all of the ingredients and whisk until smooth. Refrigerate until very cold, 4 hours or overnight. Place in ice cream freezer and freeze according to the manufacturer's directions.

Serves 4

SAUCES

BÉCHAMEL SAUCE

- 4 tablespoons butter
- 4 tablespoons flour
- 1/2 teaspoon salt
- 1/2 teaspoon cayenne pepper (optional)
- 2 cups milk

In a skillet, melt the butter. Take off the heat, add the flour, salt, and cayenne pepper, and blend well. Cook over medium heat, stirring constantly, until the roux bubbles and then 2 to 3 minutes more. In a saucepan, bring the milk nearly to a simmer. Pour it into the roux, mix well, bring to a boil, and cook, whisking constantly with a wooden spoon, for 1 to 2 minutes.

Makes 2 cups

Variation: Chicken Velouté Sauce. Make the béchamel with chicken stock instead of milk. To vary this, add sherry to taste.

MORNAY SAUCE

- 3 egg yolks, slightly beaten
- 1/4 cup heavy cream
- 2 tablespoons melted butter
- 2 cups hot béchamel sauce
- 2 tablespoons grated Swiss cheese
- 1 tablespoon grated Parmesan cheese

Mix the egg yolks, cream, and melted butter, then blend with the béchamel and cook, over low heat or in the top of a double boiler over simmering water until the sauce reaches a simmer. Add the cheeses and mix well.

Makes 3 cups

Variations: Use other cheeses, such as Monterey Jack and cheddar.

Sherry Mornay Sauce. Add sherry to taste.

SUPRÊME CREAM SAUCE

- 1 cup chicken velouté sauce
- 4 egg yolks
- About 1 cup heavy cream

Enrich the sauce with egg yolks, add cream to the desired consistency, and mix well. Keep it warm until needed. Do not overheat it or it will break.

Makes 2 cups

CHEDDAR CHEESE SAUCE

- 1 pound cheddar cheese, grated
- 2 teaspoons dry mustard
- 2 teaspoons paprika
- 1/2 cup milk
- 1 3/4 quarts béchamel sauce
- 1 1/2 teaspoons Worcestershire sauce
- 2 to 3 dashes Tabasco sauce
- Salt
- White pepper

Put the cheese, mustard, paprika, and milk in a saucepan. Mix with a wooden spoon. Add 1 cup of the béchamel and heat until cheese is melted, stirring constantly. Add the rest of the béchamel and the Worcestershire sauce and Tabasco sauce. Bring to a boil, beating constantly with a whisk. Add salt and pepper, and strain through a chinois. Use for macaroni and cheese, on pasta, with cooked vegetables, etc.

Makes 9 cups

Unlike most cheese sauces, this can be kept on hand in the freezer.

NEWBURG SAUCE

- 2 tablespoons butter
- 1 teaspoon paprika
- 1 cup dry sherry
- 3 cups béchamel sauce
- Salt
- White pepper

Melt the butter in a saucepan and cook paprika in it for 2 to 3 minutes, blending well. Add the sherry, mix, and bring to a simmer. Add the béchamel and whip briskly to mix well. Let it simmer for 5 minutes, then season with salt and pepper. Strain it through a stainless-steel screen and use for a Newburg dish.

Makes 1 quart

There is more than one way to make a good Newburg sauce. The most common is to start with a cream sauce.

The second method is definitely unusual, but effective no end. If you want the color usually seen in a Newburg sauce, add paprika to the cream in the very beginning, or add about 1 tablespoon tomato paste with the butter.

- Lobster or shrimp shells
- 1 teaspoon finely chopped shallot
- 1 teaspoon dry or semisweet sherry
- 2 cups heavy cream
- 6 egg yolks

Dry the shells in a low oven. Pulverize them, put them in a saucepan, and add the shallot and sherry. Heat the cream in the top of a double boiler, add the yolks, and stir constantly until the sauce begins to thicken. Strain the shell mixture and add the juice to the cream sauce.

Makes about 2 cups

Variation: Thermidor Sauce. Sauté mushrooms in a little butter and sherry and add it to the sauce. For lobster thermidor, put lobster meat in it, fill a lobster shell with the mixture, and bake it.

ONION CREAM SAUCE

- 4 tablespoons butter
- 4 tablespoons all-purpose flour
- 2 cups light cream
- 2 tablespoons minced onion
- 1 egg, well beaten
- 1/2 teaspoon salt
- 1 tablespoon minced fresh parsley

Heat the butter until it foams, then stir in the flour and cook for 2 to 3 minutes. Add the cream slowly, making it as thick as a béchamel sauce, or as thick as you want it to be. Add the onion. Let it all simmer for 10 minutes, then quickly whip in the egg and salt. Add the parsley and serve it under your dinner entrée.

Makes 2 cups

HOLLANDAISE SAUCE

- 2 egg yolks
- Salt
- 2 teaspoons water
- 1 cup hot clarified butter
- Lemon juice
- Dash of cayenne pepper

Remove the membrane from the egg yolks and put the yolks in a stainless-steel bowl. Add a small pinch of salt and whip slightly. As soon as the yolks darken, add the water and whip to a froth, at least doubling the volume. Cook over low heat or in the top of a double boiler until consistency reaches the soft-peaks stage. Remove from the heat and begin adding the butter, slowly to start, then faster. Add lemon juice, cayenne pepper, and salt to taste.

Makes 1 1/2 cups

BLENDER HOLLANDAISE

- 4 egg yolks
- 3 to 4 tablespoons lemon juice
- 1/4 teaspoon salt
- 1/8 teaspoon white pepper
- 2 cups melted butter

In a blender, combine the egg yolks, lemon juice, and salt and pepper. In a saucepan, heat the butter until it bubbles. Turn on the blender and gradually pour in the hot butter, blending until thick and smooth.

Makes 2 cups

BÉARNAISE SAUCE

- 2 fresh tarragon leaves
- 4 tablespoons tarragon wine vinegar
- 2 cups hollandaise sauce

Chop the tarragon and toss with the vinegar. In a skillet, bring to a boil, then turn the heat down low and cook until the liquid is evaporated. Whip into the hollandaise sauce.

Makes 2 cups

MARCHAND DE VINS BUTTER

- 2 shallots, minced
- 3/4 cup dry red wine
- 1 teaspoon glace de viande (available from L. J. Minor Corp.)
- Pepper
- 4 teaspoons butter, softened
- 2 tablespoons minced fresh parsley
- Juice of 1 lemon

Put the shallots and wine in a small saucepan and cook until wine has almost evaporated. Stir in the glace de viande and pepper and swirl in the butter. Cook briefly to the desired consistency. Add the parsley and lemon juice, and serve over steak.

Makes 1 cup

PIQUANT SAUCE

- 4 ounces dill pickles
- 8 ounces onions
- 1 stick (8 tablespoons) butter
- 1 quart brown sauce (base available from L. J. Minor Corp.)
- 1/2 pint cider vinegar
- 2 tablespoons dry red wine
- 2 tablespoons chopped fresh parsley

Chop the pickles. Mince the onions, heat the butter in a large saucepan, and sauté the minced onion briefly; do not let it brown. Add the brown sauce, vinegar, and wine, and simmer for at least 30 minutes. Add the pickle and cook for 15 minutes more. Remove it from the heat, add the parsley, and refrigerate until needed.

Makes 2 quarts

MADEIRA SAUCE

- 1 cup brown sauce (base available from L. J. Minor Corp.)
- 1/2 cup Madeira

Bring the brown sauce to a boil in a large saucepan, then let it simmer until reduced to about three fourths its original volume. Add the Madeira and let it simmer for another 5 minutes. Strain through cheesecloth or a fine strainer and refrigerate until needed.

Makes about 1 1/2 cups

BARBECUE SAUCE

- 1 cup oil
- 2 1/2 cups finely blended onions
- 3 1/2 cups finely blended celery
- 1 1/2 cups brown sugar
- 3 teaspoons salt
- 5 cups ketchup
- 1/2 cup red wine vinegar
- 1 pint pineapple juice
- 5 tablespoons prepared mustard
- 5 tablespoons Worcestershire sauce
- 2 pints water

Heat the oil and sauté the onions and celery until just done. Add the remaining ingredients and simmer for 30 minutes. Use hot or cold.

Makes 2 quarts

Freeze what you don't use now.

JOHNNY REB'S BARBECUE SAUCE

- 2 tablespoons butter
- 1 cup finely chopped onion
- 1 cup diced celery
- 1 teaspoon prepared mustard
- 1 tablespoon lemon juice
- 1/4 cup water
- 1/2 teaspoon cayenne pepper
- 1/2 teaspoon salt
- 2 teaspoons liquid smoke (optional)
- 1 cup tomato sauce
- 1 tablespoon brown sugar
- 1 tablespoon cider vinegar
- 1 tablespoon chili powder
- Pinch of ground cloves
- 1/8 teaspoon pepper

In a medium saucepan, melt the butter over medium heat. Add the onion and sauté until golden brown. Stir in the remaining ingredients and heat to a boil. Reduce the heat and simmer, uncovered, stirring occasionally, for about 30 minutes.

Makes 2 cups

CHEF RENÉ'S BARBECUED PIG SAUCE

- 4 tablespoons butter
- 2 medium onions, chopped
- 2 tablespoons prepared mustard
- 1/2 cup water
- 1 teaspoon salt
- 4 cups tomato sauce
- 1 medium-size can tomato juice
- 2 teaspoons cider vinegar
- 2 tablespoons chili powder
- 1/4 teaspoon pepper
- 2 cups diced celery
- 2 tablespoons lemon juice
- 1 teaspoon cayenne pepper
- 4 cups bottled chili sauce
- 2 teaspoons brown sugar
- 2 teaspoons red wine vinegar
- Pinch of ground cloves
- 1 cup dry white wine

In a large pot, melt the butter over medium heat. Add the onions and sauté until golden brown. Mix in the remaining ingredients and bring to a boil. Reduce the heat to a simmer and cook, uncovered, for about 30 minutes. Use it to baste the pig, especially the inside. (Keep the pig as moist as possible, but do not worry about the skin, which will become very crisp and dark, as it is usually not eaten. Test the pig for doneness at the thickest part of the meat at the shoulder area, inside. Once you see a complete release of clear juices, it is done to perfection.)

Makes 1 gallon

PROVENÇAL TOMATO SAUCE

- Olive oil
- 1 garlic clove, crushed
- 1 quart chopped or crushed tomatoes
- 1 small bay leaf
- 1 onion, chopped
- 1 large carrot, chopped
- 1 celery stalk, chopped
- Bouquet garni (thyme, sage, bay leaf, allspice)
- Salt
- Pepper
- Sugar

Heat oil and sauté the garlic. Add the tomatoes, bay leaf, onion, carrot, celery, and bouquet garni. Cover the pan and simmer for 30 minutes. Remove the bouquet garni and bay leaf, and season with salt, pepper, and sugar to taste. Either sieve the sauce or purée it in a blender. Serve over or under steak au poivre.

Makes about 1 quart

MARINADE FOR LAMB SHISH KEBAB

- 1 cup olive oil
- 1/2 cup salad oil
- 4 tablespoons vinegar
- 2 tablespoons lemon juice
- 1/2 teaspoon chopped garlic
- 1 1/4 teaspoons salt
- 1 large pinch of marjoram
- Thyme
- Oregano

Mix together and marinate the lamb for 4 hours to overnight.
Makes about 2 cups

Save the marinade and reuse it. It will keep, refrigerated, for six months.

POULETTE SAUCE D'ANN

- 1 quart chicken stock
- 1/2 onion, chopped
- 2 large mushrooms, thinly sliced
- 2 tablespoons Chablis
- 2 black olives
- Salt
- White pepper

Heat the stock and cook the onions and mushrooms in it. Reduce the stock by one fourth. Add the Chablis and olives and season, but be careful with the salt. Boil briefly. If the sauce seems too thin, strain it and reserve the solids; bring the sauce to a boil and reduce it still more. Put the onion and mushroom mixture back in, heat through, and serve with chicken.
Makes 1 quart

CHICKEN WING SAUCE

- 1 quart chicken stock
- 2 onions, finely minced
- 2 carrots, finely minced
- 2 stalks celery, finely minced
- 4 tablespoons dark soy sauce
- 1 cup brown sugar
- 2 tablespoons Worcestershire sauce
- 4 tablespoons red wine vinegar
- 1 teaspoon grated fresh ginger

Heat the chicken stock and in it cook the minced onion, carrot, and celery. Add the remaining ingredients and let simmer for 5 to 10 minutes. Use to marinate and cook chicken wings.
Makes 1 quart

SWEET AND SOUR SAUCE

- 3 cups chicken stock
- 1 cup honey
- 1 cup brown sugar
- 1½ to 2 cups white wine vinegar
- 2 garlic cloves, finely minced
- 4 tablespoons lemon juice
- 2 teaspoons glace de viande (available from L. J. Minor Corp.) or Bovril
- Large pinch of cayenne pepper
- 4 tablespoons cornstarch
- 4 tablespoons soy sauce
- ½ cup semisweet sherry
- 12 tablespoons water

Heat the stock, add the honey and sugar, and stir to dissolve. Add the vinegar, garlic, lemon juice, glace de viande, and cayenne pepper. In a bowl, blend together the cornstarch, soy sauce, sherry, and water. Add this to the pot, and stir until the sauce thickens. Serve with cooked chicken.

Serves 8 to 12

Variation: Add pineapple chunks and small pieces of boiled or sautéed green pepper, and use pineapple juice instead of water.

This wonderful sauce keeps for three months in the refrigerator and comes in handy for leftovers.

ANN GODE'S VEAL SAUCE

- 2 tablespoons flour
- 2 tablespoons butter
- 1 cup veal stock (deglaze a veal-cooking pan)
- ¼ cup dry white wine
- 1 cup heavy cream
- 8 each black and green olives, coarsely chopped
- 2 hard-boiled eggs, chopped
- Salt
- Crushed peppercorns

In a saucepan, cook the flour in frothing-hot butter for 2 to 3 minutes and add the stock and wine. When the mixture thickens, add the cream slowly, then the olives and eggs. Add salt and peppercorns to taste. Serve with veal.

Serves 4

CREOLE SAUCE

- Oil or bacon fat
- 1 pound celery, cut into julienne
- 1 1/4 pounds peppers, seeded and cut into julienne
- 1 pound onions, cut into julienne
- 8 ounces mushrooms, cut into julienne
- 2 garlic cloves, crushed
- 2 tablespoons flour
- 1 1-pound 12-ounce can tomatoes, in chunks or crushed
- 1 1-pound 12-ounce can tomato purée
- 1 quart beef stock
- 1 teaspoon crushed red pepper
- Scant 1 teaspoon salt
- 1 bay leaf

Heat oil or bacon fat and sauté all the vegetables, but do not let them brown. Add the flour to this and cook as for a roux. Add the tomatoes, purée, stock, and seasonings. Cook until the vegetables are done but not browned. Serve over fish.

Makes 2 quarts

Note: If you want the sauce to be hot and spicy, add a bit of Paul Prudhomme's Seafood Magic Seasoning. For dishes other than fish, use Nellie's Cajun Seasoning, from St. Paul, Minnesota—one of the best I have tried.

Make up a gallon and store in the freezer, or cut the recipe in half. Buy mild peppers or a mixture of mild and hot, as you like.

FISH SAUCE I

- 1 tablespoon butter
- 1 carrot, finely chopped
- 1 onion, finely chopped
- 1/2 cup heavy cream
- 1/2 cup dry white wine
- 2 cups fish stock (base available from L. J. Minor Corp.), heated
- Salt
- Pepper

Melt the butter and sauté the carrot and onion. Add the cream and wine and cook until thick. Add to the fish stock and season to taste.

Serves 6 to 8

FISH SAUCE II

- 1 carrot, finely minced
- 1/2 medium onion, finely chopped
- 1 tablespoon butter
- 1/2 tablespoon flour
- 1/2 cup sauterne
- 1/2 cup heavy cream
- Salt
- Pepper

Sauté the carrot and onion in butter until soft but not browned. Add the flour and cook for 2 to 3 minutes. Add the sauterne and boil briefly, then the cream, salt, and pepper. Heat through, pour over the fish, and bake until the fish is cooked.

Serves 4

This makes enough for about 2 pounds of fish.

PESTO I

- 2 cups stemmed fresh basil
- 1 cup olive oil
- 2 large tablespoons minced garlic
- 1/4 cup pine nuts
- Salt

Process the basil leaves in a food processor fitted with the metal blade, or pound them using a mortar and pestle. Slowly add the olive oil, and process or stir until the mixture becomes pastelike. Add the garlic and blend well. Stir in the pine nuts and add salt to taste. Toss with hot or cold pasta, or serve with potatoes or hot or cold broiled fish.

Serves 4 to 8

PESTO II

- 1 cup fresh white bread crumbs (crusts trimmed)
- 1/4 cup dry white wine
- 2 cups fresh basil
- 3 garlic cloves
- 1/2 cup pine nuts
- 1 teaspoon salt
- 1 cup oil
- 1/2 cup grated Parmesan cheese
- 3 tablespoons grated Romano cheese

In a saucepan, combine the bread crumbs and wine and stir over low heat until the mixture becomes a smooth paste. Let cool. Put it in a blender with the basil, garlic, pine nuts, and salt, and mix at high speed until thick and creamy, about 1 to 2 minutes. Add the oil in a steady stream, almost drop by drop at first, and blend until smooth and well mixed. Pour into a bowl and gently stir in the two cheeses.

Makes 3 cups

If you keep this pesto in the refrigerator or freezer, you can easily give a fresh flavor to long-cooked dishes. Form it into small balls and use sparingly in, for example, minestrone.

CURRY POWDER

Curry powder, although long considered one of the most popular spices in the world, is from India but is not a true spice. It is made up of many—for example, turmeric, fenugreek, ginger, red and green chilies, cumin, cardamom, nutmeg, cinnamon, cloves, lemon grass, and curry leaves. In India each family makes its own, according to taste, and sautés it in clarified butter to intensify the flavors. When cooking Indian or curry dishes, if you want a *stronger* flavor, just use a bit more curry; for a *spicier* flavor, add more red pepper.

MINT SAUCE

- 1 cup fresh mint
- 1/2 cup cider vinegar
- 6 tablespoons sugar
- 1 1/2 cups water
- 1 12-ounce jar mint sauce

Chop the mint. Put the mint, vinegar, sugar, and water in a pot and bring to a boil. Let simmer for 10 to 20 minutes. Add mint sauce to thin it out, using to taste, and serve with lamb.

Serves 4

MAYONNAISE

- 1/2 teaspoon salt
- 2 tablespoons lemon juice
- 2 tablespoons vinegar
- 1/8 teaspoon cayenne pepper
- 1/8 teaspoon paprika
- 1 heaping tablespoon Dijon mustard
- 4 egg yolks, at room temperature
- 2 cups peanut oil, or 1 cup peanut oil plus 1 cup vegetable oil

In a small bowl, dissolve the salt in the lemon juice and vinegar. Add the cayenne, paprika, mustard, and egg yolks. Stir until smooth. Slowly add the oil in a thin stream, almost drop by drop, stirring quickly with a wire whisk. Taste for seasoning.

Use immediately, or stir in 1 to 2 tablespoons boiling water and keep under refrigeration in a tightly covered container.

Makes 2 1/2 cups

Variations: Blender Mayonnaise. Combine the first seven ingredients and 1/2 cup oil in the blender. Cover and run at low speed just until blended. Remove the cover and add the remaining oil in a slow, steady stream, drop by drop at first.

Dijon Sauce (for eggs, fish, beef, poultry, and shellfish). Make mayonnaise well endowed with Dijon mustard.

Gribiche Sauce (for shellfish and cold fish). Prepare mayonnaise with very finely chopped hard-boiled egg yolks (instead of raw yolks), seasoned and blended with vinegar and oil. Fold in chopped gherkins, capers, and the whites of hard-boiled eggs.

Green Sauce (for eggs, fish, shellfish, oysters, and vegetables). Make mayonnaise with chopped fines herbs (parsley, chives, tarragon), onion juice, and blanched, drained watercress and spinach, then perfume it with a touch of Pernod.

Tartar Sauce (for fried or broiled fish or shellfish and egg salads). Add prepared mustard and anchovy paste, or chopped pickle and lemon juice.

Aurora Sauce (for eggs, shellfish, vegetables, fish, and meat). Enhance mayonnaise with tomato purée.

Russian Sauce (for shellfish, oysters, clams). Add tomato purée, chili sauce, horseradish, and chopped celery.

To think of mayonnaise only as a sandwich spread or a salad dressing is to do it a supreme disservice. It is a classic and traditional sauce. During the summer, a cold dish accented by a cold mayonnaise sauce is refreshing, easy to digest, and highly palatable.

As with any sauce or dish, high-quality ingredients are a necessity. I find the traditional choice, olive oil, too strong for mayonnaise. I prefer peanut oil, and a half-and-half blend of peanut oil and corn oil is even lighter.

The choice of acid, too, is a matter of taste. It may be white or red wine vinegar, tarragon or cider vinegar, fresh lemon juice, or a half-and-half combination. Whether you use dry mustard or Dijon, white pepper, cayenne pepper, or a dash of a liquid hot condiment sauce, each ingredient will lend its distinctive personality to the sauce. Equal amounts of salt and sugar strike a tangy note.

The seasoning in a perfect mayonnaise should be harmonious and the texture tender yet thick. The extra time it takes to make mayonnaise by hand instead of in a blender is only minutes compared to seconds. Something magical happens when you try it by hand—your work, your creation, becomes a part, or perhaps an extension, of yourself, which contributes to the pleasure of making and serving it.

For perfect mayonnaise, follow these rules:

1. All ingredients must be at room temperature.

2. The fresher the eggs, the better the mayonnaise will be. Discard the chalaza (membrane attached to shell) and any gelatinous white threads from the yolks.

3. Dissolve the salt and sugar (if you're using sugar) in the acid, then mix it into the yolks with the other basic ingredients before you start incorporating the oil.

4. Incorporate the first few tablespoons of oil drop by drop, encouraging a good emulsion to form. Then add the rest of the oil in a very thin stream (still almost drop by drop), stirring or whisking constantly.

5. Remember that 2 large Grade A egg yolks can absorb 1 cup of oil, so 2 yolks per cup of oil plus 2 tablespoons vinegar and/or lemon juice is the correct ratio.

6. The smaller the quantity of mayonnaise, the smaller the bowl must be, and vice versa. Use a whisk in proportion to the size of the bowl.

7. Never use black pepper in any clear, white, or light-colored sauce.

8. A tablespoon of hot liquid briskly stirred in at the end will help stabilize the emulsion. This will thin the sauce at first, but it will thicken on standing.

9. If the mayonnaise curdles or separates, put 1 slightly beaten egg yolk in a clean bowl and, using a clean whisk, gradually beat in the curdled mayonnaise as though it were oil—drop by drop until it is smooth, then in a steady stream.

RÉMOULADE SAUCE I

- 1 cup mayonnaise
- 1 tablespoon chopped fresh parsley
- 2 tablespoons Dijon mustard
- 1 teaspoon paprika
- Dash of Tabasco sauce
- 1 tablespoon vinegar
- 1 tablespoon chopped onion
- 1 tablespoon chopped celery
- 1 tablespoon prepared horseradish
- 1/2 teaspoon salt
- 1/4 cup salad oil
- 1/2 teaspoon Worcestershire sauce

Combine all of the ingredients in a small bowl and mix until well blended. Refrigerate for several hours or overnight. Serve with shrimp, crab meat, etc.

Makes 1 1/2 cups

RÉMOULADE SAUCE II

- 2 cups mayonnaise
- 1 tablespoon minced sour pickles (preferably French cornichons)
- 1 tablespoon grated onion
- 1/2 teaspoon anchovy paste
- 2 tablespoons minced capers
- 1 to 2 tablespoons Dijon mustard
- 2 teaspoons each minced fresh parsley, tarragon, and chervil, or 1 teaspoon each of the dried herbs

Blend all of the ingredients and use when chilled.

Makes 2 1/2 cups

CUCUMBER SAUCE

- 3 large firm cucumbers, peeled and cut lengthwise
- Juice of 1 lemon
- 1 tablespoon gelatin, softened in 1/4 cup cold water
- 1 tablespoon salt
- Dash of Tabasco sauce
- 1 1/2 teaspoons Worcestershire sauce
- 1/2 cup mayonnaise (page 255)
- 2 generous tablespoons sour cream
- 1 cup heavy cream
- Dill or dill seeds (optional)

Use a spoon to scrape out the cucumber seeds. Blanch the cucumbers in boiling water with lemon juice for 3 minutes.

Drain and purée in a blender or food processor until smooth. Add the gelatin to the hot cucumber purée and stir until dissolved. Pour the mixture into a bowl and season with salt, Tabasco sauce, and Worcestershire sauce. Set the bowl over ice and stir until the mixture becomes cold and begins to set, 3 to 4 minutes. Whisk in the mayonnaise. In another bowl, beat the sour cream and heavy cream until almost firm; add it to the cucumber mixture, stirring until smooth. Add dill to taste. Pour into a serving bowl and refrigerate for at least 1 hour.

Makes 1 quart

Serve this with vegetables or fish, especially salmon. If the cucumbers are not waxed, there is no need to peel them.

MALTESE SAUCE

- 1/2 cup port
- 1 tablespoon gelatin, softened in 1/4 cup cold water
- 1 6-ounce can frozen orange juice concentrate, thawed
- 1 cup heavy cream, firmly whipped
- 1/2 cup mayonnaise made without mustard
- Grated zest of 1 orange

In a small saucepan over medium heat, cook the port for 5 to 10 minutes, until it is reduced to 2 tablespoons. Add the gelatin and stir to melt. Stir in the orange juice concentrate. Pour the mixture over the whipped cream and blend. Fold in the mayonnaise. Garnish with orange zest and chill.

Makes 3 cups

Serve this sauce with avocados or carrots, or fruit such as apples and grapefruit, perhaps combined with walnuts.

BRANDIED CREAM SAUCE

- 1 cup double or heavy cream
- 1/4 cup plain yogurt
- 1/4 cup sour cream
- 1 tablespoon sugar
- 1 jigger brandy

Whip the double cream just until stiff and mix in the remaining ingredients (adjust the amounts to achieve the desired consistency).

Makes 1 1/2 cups

This sauce has numerous uses—for example, spread it on a dessert plate and place cut-up fresh fruit on top, or use it under puff pastry filled with cooked fruit.

Salad Dressings

*M*ost salad dressings have as basic ingredients oil, vinegar, and some type of seasoning.

FRENCH DRESSING

- 1 teaspoon salt
- 1/8 teaspoon pepper
- 1/2 cup tarragon vinegar
- 1/2 teaspoon prepared mustard or 1/8 teaspoon dry mustard
- 1 1/2 cups olive oil
- 1/2 tablespoon each chopped fresh basil, thyme, marjoram, and chervil

Just mix.
Makes 2 cups

ITALIAN DRESSING

- 1 cup olive oil
- 1/2 cup red wine vinegar
- 2 teaspoons Italian seasoning
- 2 garlic cloves, crushed
- 1/4 to 1/2 teaspoon crushed black pepper

Combine and mix well.
Makes 1 1/2 cups

BLUE CHEESE DRESSING

- 3/4 cup oil
- 1/2 pint sour cream
- Very finely chopped scallion stems
- 3 ounces blue cheese
- 1/4 cup white or red wine vinegar, or more to taste
- Juice of 1/2 lemon
- 1/2 garlic clove, pressed or minced
- Small pinch each of marjoram and chopped dill

Mix all of the ingredients, leaving the cheese rather lumpy—the way most people like it.

Makes 2 cups

Variations: Change the cheese to Roquefort or cheddar, Swiss, etc.

You can also change the flavorings: use celery seed, savory, chives, lime juice, yogurt, salt and pepper. Use tarragon or apple cider vinegar.

SPINACH SALAD DRESSING

- 1/4 cup French dressing
- 1/4 cup Italian dressing
- 1/2 cup mayonnaise
- 1 tablespoon white wine
- 1/2 teaspoon lemon juice
- Large garlic clove, minced
- White pepper
- 2 hard-boiled eggs, chopped

Combine all of the ingredients and mix well.

Makes about 1 1/2 cups

BASIL DRESSING

- 1/2 cup olive oil
- 2 1/2 tablespoons finely chopped fresh basil or 1 tablespoon crumbled dried basil
- 2 teaspoons sugar
- 1/2 teaspoon salt
- 1/4 cup red wine vinegar
- 2 large garlic cloves, minced
- 1/2 teaspoon black pepper

Mix by hand or in a blender. Refrigerate until ready to use.

Makes about 1 cup

This also goes well with spinach salad.

RAW VEGETABLE SAUCE

- 1 quart mayonnaise
- 2 teaspoons prepared horseradish
- 2 garlic cloves, crushed
- 1/2 teaspoon curry powder
- Dash of Tabasco sauce
- 4 teaspoons Worcestershire sauce
- 1/2 onion, grated
- 1 tablespoon celery seed
- 2 tablespoons prepared mustard
- Pepper

Mix together and serve as a sauce or dip.

Makes 3 pints

SHRIMP COCKTAIL SAUCE

- 1 large jar chili sauce
- Juice of 2 lemons
- 1 bottle ketchup
- 3/4 cup prepared horseradish

Mix the ingredients to your taste, bearing in mind that the horseradish can make it very strong.

Makes 1 quart

FRESH FRUIT SALAD DRESSING

- 1 pint heavy cream
- 1/2 pint sour cream
- 6 shakes vanilla extract
- 1 tablespoon sugar
- 1 to 2 jiggers brandy

Whip the cream and blend in the sour cream, vanilla extract, sugar, and brandy.

Makes about 1 quart

APPENDIX

EQUIVALENTS

Volume Measures

60 drops = 1 teaspoon
3 teaspoons = 1 tablespoon
2 tablespoons = 1 fluid ounce or 1/8 cup
4 tablespoons = 1/4 cup
5 1/3 tablespoons = 1/3 cup
8 tablespoons = 1/2 cup or 4 ounces or 1 gill or 1 teacup
16 tablespoons = 1 cup or 8 ounces
3/8 cup = 1/4 cup plus 2 tablespoons
5/8 cup = 1/2 cup plus 2 tablespoons
7/8 cup = 3/4 cup plus 2 tablespoons
1 cup = 1/2 pint or 8 ounces
2 cups = 1 pint
1 quart = 2 pints
1 gallon = 4 quarts
1 peck = 2 gallons
1 bushel = 4 pecks

Miscellaneous

A few grains or a speck = less than 1/8 teaspoon
Pinch = As much as can be picked up between the tip of one finger and the thumb. A large pinch = two fingers and the thumb.
1 jigger = 2 ounces
1 minim = 1 drop
A dash = 10 drops
1 teaspoon = 6 dashes

Weight or Avoirdupois Equivalents

1 ounce = 16 drams
1 pound = 16 ounces
1 kilo = 2.2 pounds

FLOUR

For 1 cup sifted all-purpose flour, you can use any of the following (sifted):

1 cup cake flour plus 2 tablespoons all-purpose flour
1/3 cup cornmeal plus 2/3 cup flour
1/2 cup cornmeal plus 1/2 cup flour
1/2 cup bran plus 1/2 cup flour
3/4 cup bran plus 1/4 cup flour
1/2 cup rye flour plus 1/2 cup flour
1/2 cup whole-wheat flour plus 1/2 cup flour
3/4 cup whole-wheat flour plus 1/4 cup flour

SUGAR

For 1 cup granulated sugar, you can use:

1 cup brown sugar, well packed
3/4 cup honey and reduce the liquid by 3 tablespoons
2 cups corn syrup and reduce the liquid by 1/2 cup
1 1/2 cups maple syrup and reduce the liquid by 1/2 cup
1 1/2 cups molasses and reduce the liquid by 6 tablespoons

A COMPARISON OF THICKENING AGENTS

Thickener	Appearance	Amount	Use	Technique
Flour	Opaque	1 tablespoon per cup of liquid	Thin gravy, soup, or sauce.	Flour may be blended with fat in a roux or beurre manié or blended with liquid in a slurry or paste. Heat to 194° or above for maximum thickness and cook for several minutes to avoid a raw taste. Heating with acids causes thinning, and high sugar content reduces thickening power.
		2 tablespoons per cup of liquid	Medium gravy, soup, or sauce.	
		3 tablespoons per cup of liquid	Thick gravy, soup, or sauce.	
Browned flour	Opaque	2 tablespoons in place of 1 tablespoon white flour	Same as above; darker color, more flavor.	Same as above.
Cornstarch	Transparent	1 tablespoon in place of 2 tablespoons white flour	Sauces, fruit glazes, Chinese cooking.	Same as flour, but do not boil more than 3 minutes. Boil 1 minute to coagulate. Add acid or sugar only after coagulation.
Arrowroot	Transparent, sparkling	Variable; usually 1 tablespoon in place of 2 tablespoons white flour	Fruit sauces, delicate sauces, soups, gravies.	Attains maximum thickening at 158° to 176°. High sustained heat and stirring will cause thinning.
Potato starch	Translucent	1 tablespoon in place of 2 to 2 1/2 tablespoons white flour	Gravies, savory sauces.	Same as arrowroot.
Eggs	Opaque	2 eggs will thicken 1 cup liquid	Custards, soups, sauces.	Blend with sugar or cream first, add hot liquid to egg mixture to heat slowly and raise coagulation point, then incorporate into sauce or soup. Do not boil unless sauce includes flour.

INDEX

The information in parentheses reflects the origin or the originator of the recipe.